This Fun Workbook Belongs To:

100 SIGHT WORDS KINDERGARTEN WORKBOOK

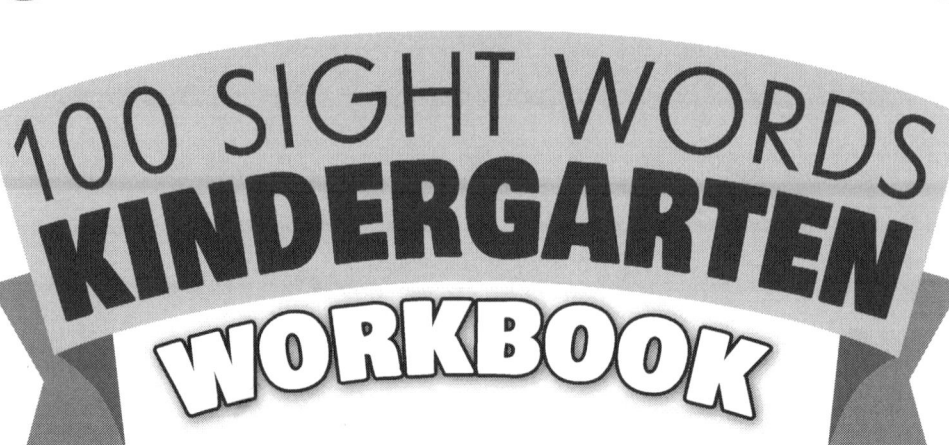

Lovingly Published by Big Dreams Art Supplies

Copyright © 2020 Big Dreams Art Supplies

BigDreamsArtSupplies.com

Illustrated by Davor Ratkovic

Printed in the United States of America

one

Trace the word and say it aloud!

one one one one one

Write the word:

Complete the sentence with the word:

I have ☐ ball.

Grab a crayon and color the shapes with the word!

one | one | two | seven | three | six | one | one | five | one | one | four

two

Trace the word and say it aloud!

two two two two two two

Write the word:

Complete the sentence with the word:

The T-rex has ☐ arms.

Grab a crayon and color the shapes with the word!

three two two one four five seven two two six

three

Trace the word and say it aloud!

three three three three

Write the word:

Complete the sentence with the word:

That bike has ▢ wheels.

Grab a crayon and color the shapes with the word!

two · two · seven · six · three · three · three · eight · four · five

four

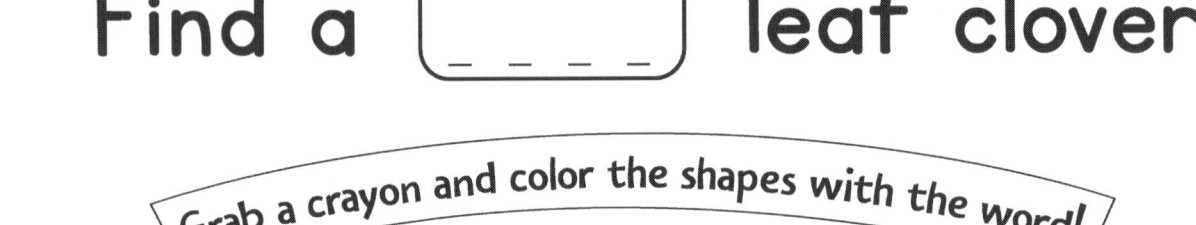

Trace the word and say it aloud!

four four four four four

Write the word:

Complete the sentence with the word:

Find a ____ leaf clover.

Grab a crayon and color the shapes with the word!

two   four   four
six   one
four   five
seven   four   three

five

Trace the word and say it aloud!

five   five   five   five

Write the word:

_____
_____
_____

Complete the sentence with the word:

There are [_ _ _ _] apples in a box.

Grab a crayon and color the shapes with the word!

three   five   five   five   two   five   six   one   six   four   five

six

Trace the word and say it aloud!

six six six six six six six

Write the word:

Complete the sentence with the word:

The ice cream has ☐ scoops.

Grab a crayon and color the shapes with the word!

one six three four six two six five seven six six

seven

Trace the word and say it aloud!

seven seven seven seven

Write the word:

Complete the sentence with the word:

I have _____ balloons.

Grab a crayon and color the shapes with the word!

one, six, three, seven, seven, seven, four, two, seven, five, seven, seven

eight

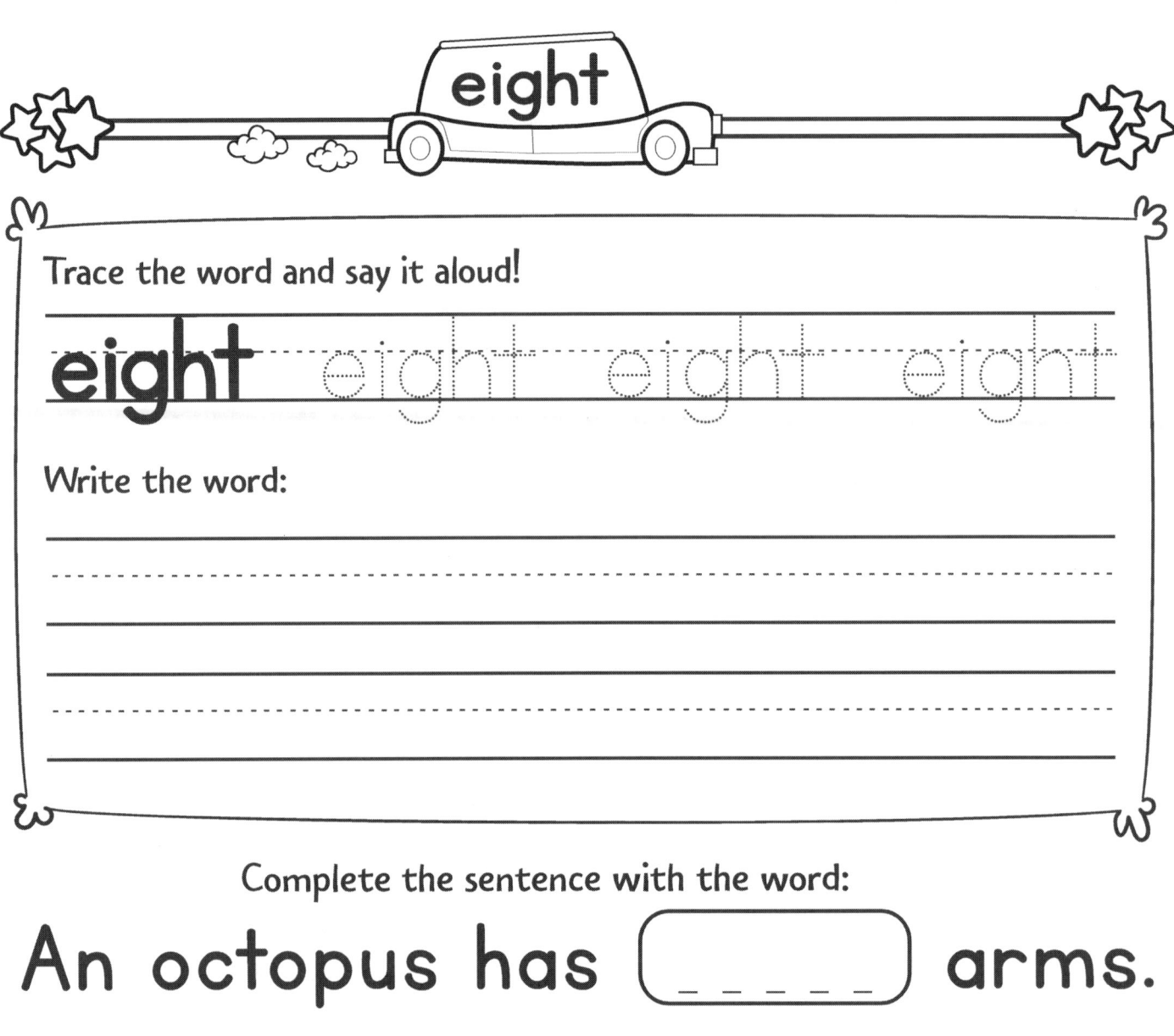

Trace the word and say it aloud!

eight eight eight eight

Write the word:

Complete the sentence with the word:

An octopus has [_ _ _ _ _] arms.

Grab a crayon and color the shapes with the word!

five eight one four three eight six eight eight two eight eight nine

Trace the word and say it aloud!

nine nine nine nine nine

Write the word:

Complete the sentence with the word:

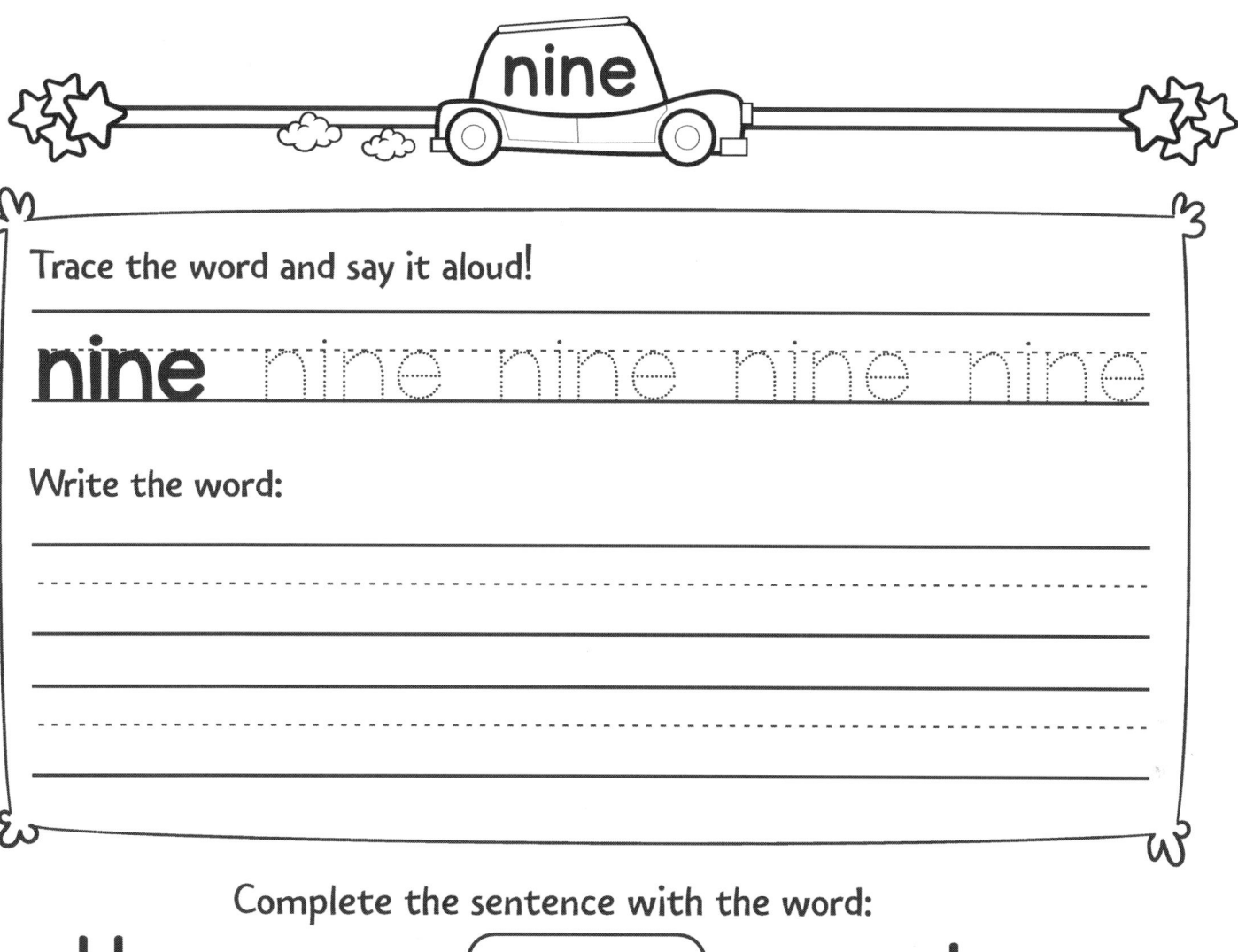

Here are ____ monsters.

Grab a crayon and color the shapes with the word!

six
four
two
nine
nine
nine
nine
nine
five
nine
one
three
nine

ten

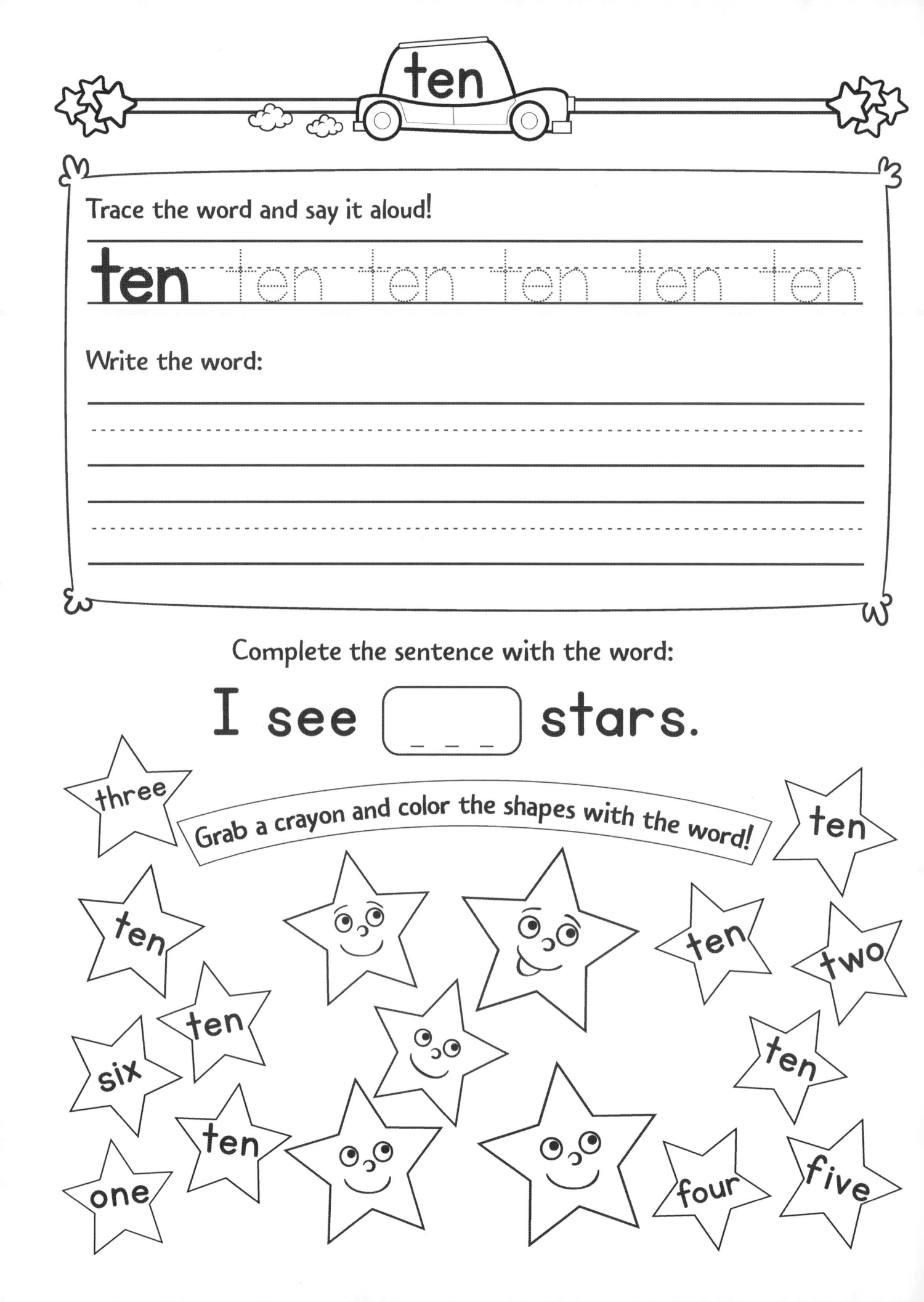

Trace the word and say it aloud!

ten ten ten ten ten ten

Write the word:

Complete the sentence with the word:

I see ☐ stars.

Grab a crayon and color the shapes with the word!

three ten
ten ten two
six ten ten
ten
one four five

black

Trace the word and say it aloud!

black black black black

Write the word:

Complete the sentence with the word:

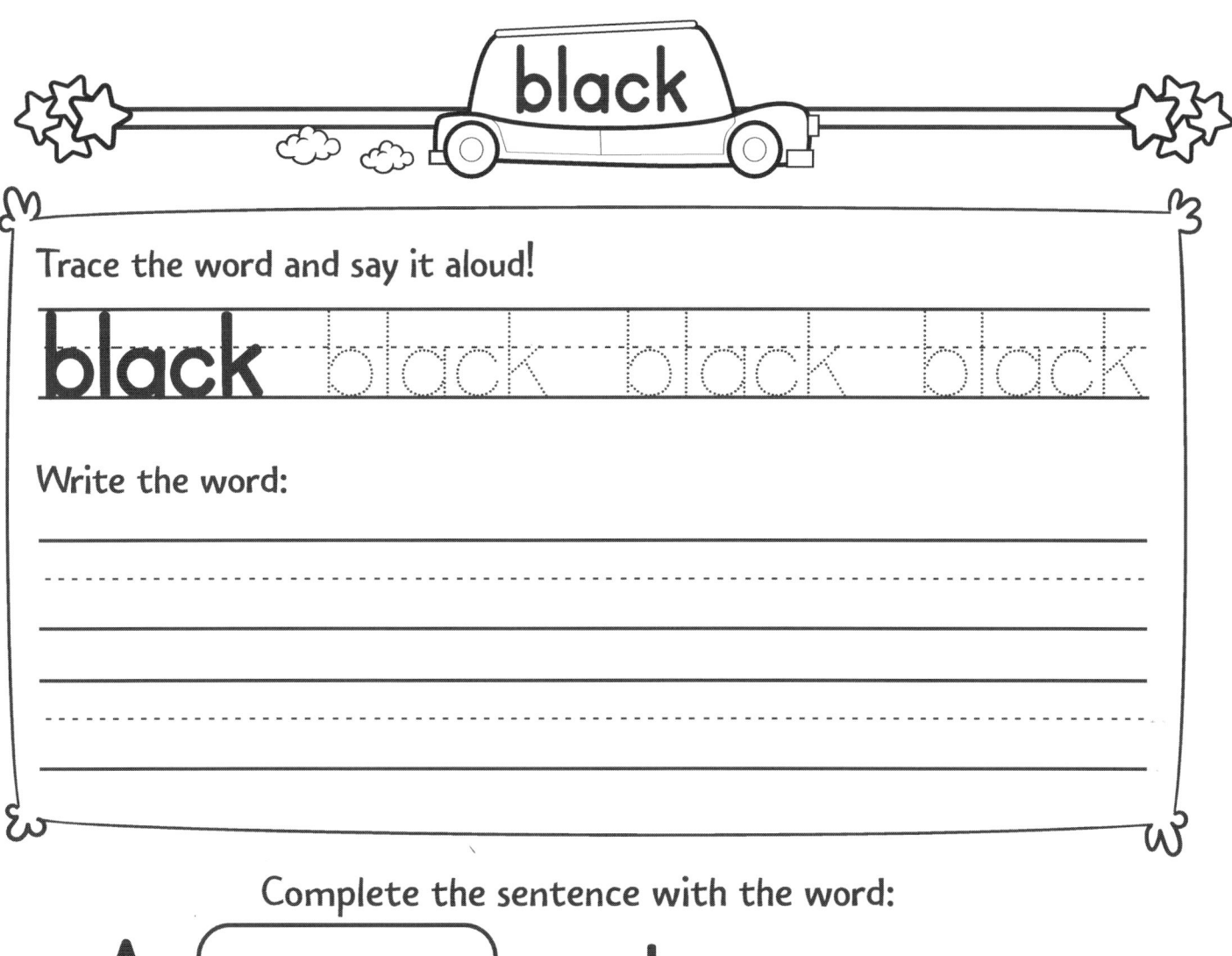

A ▢ cat ran away.

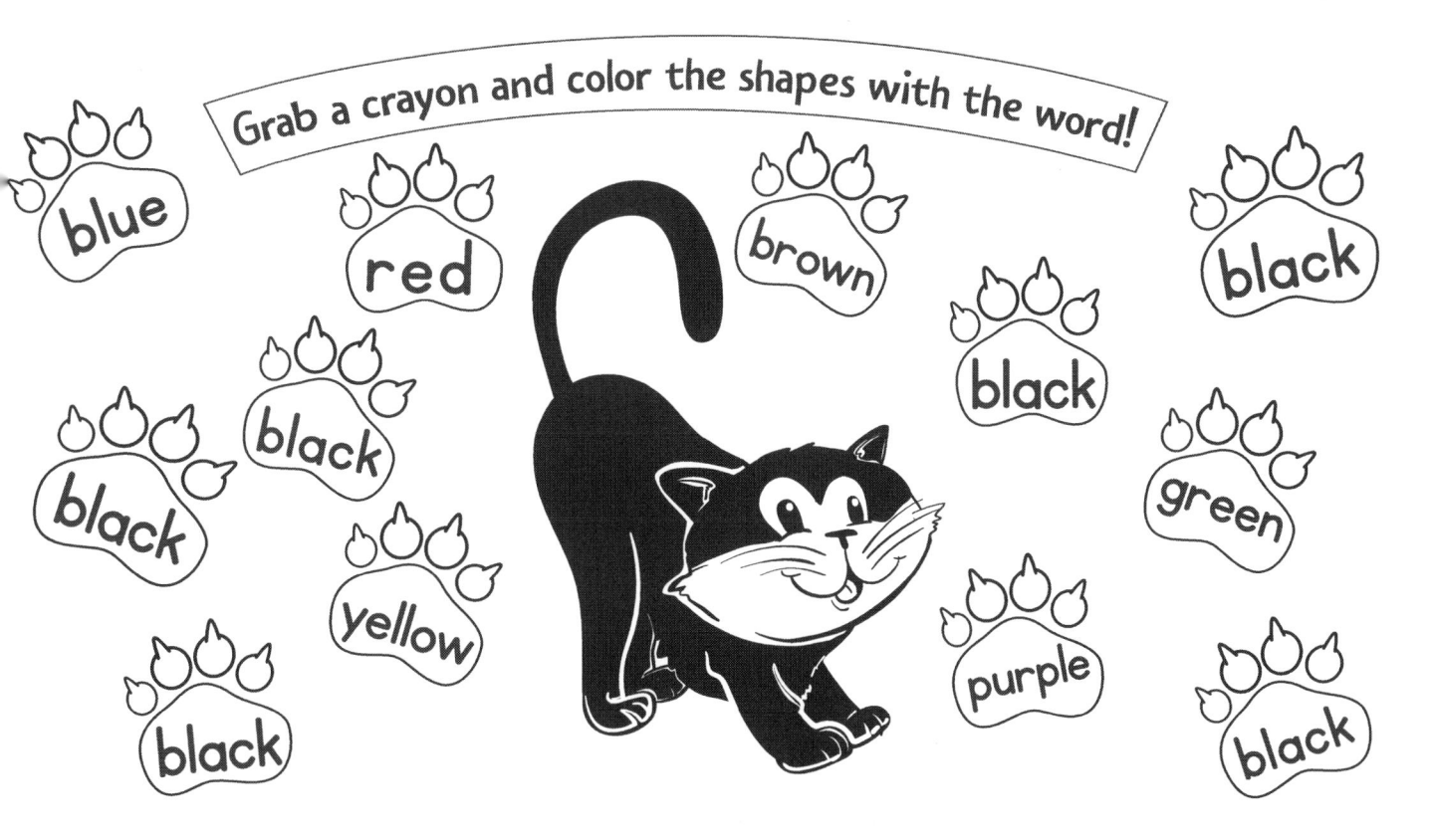

Grab a crayon and color the shapes with the word!

blue red brown black
black black
black yellow green
black purple black

blue

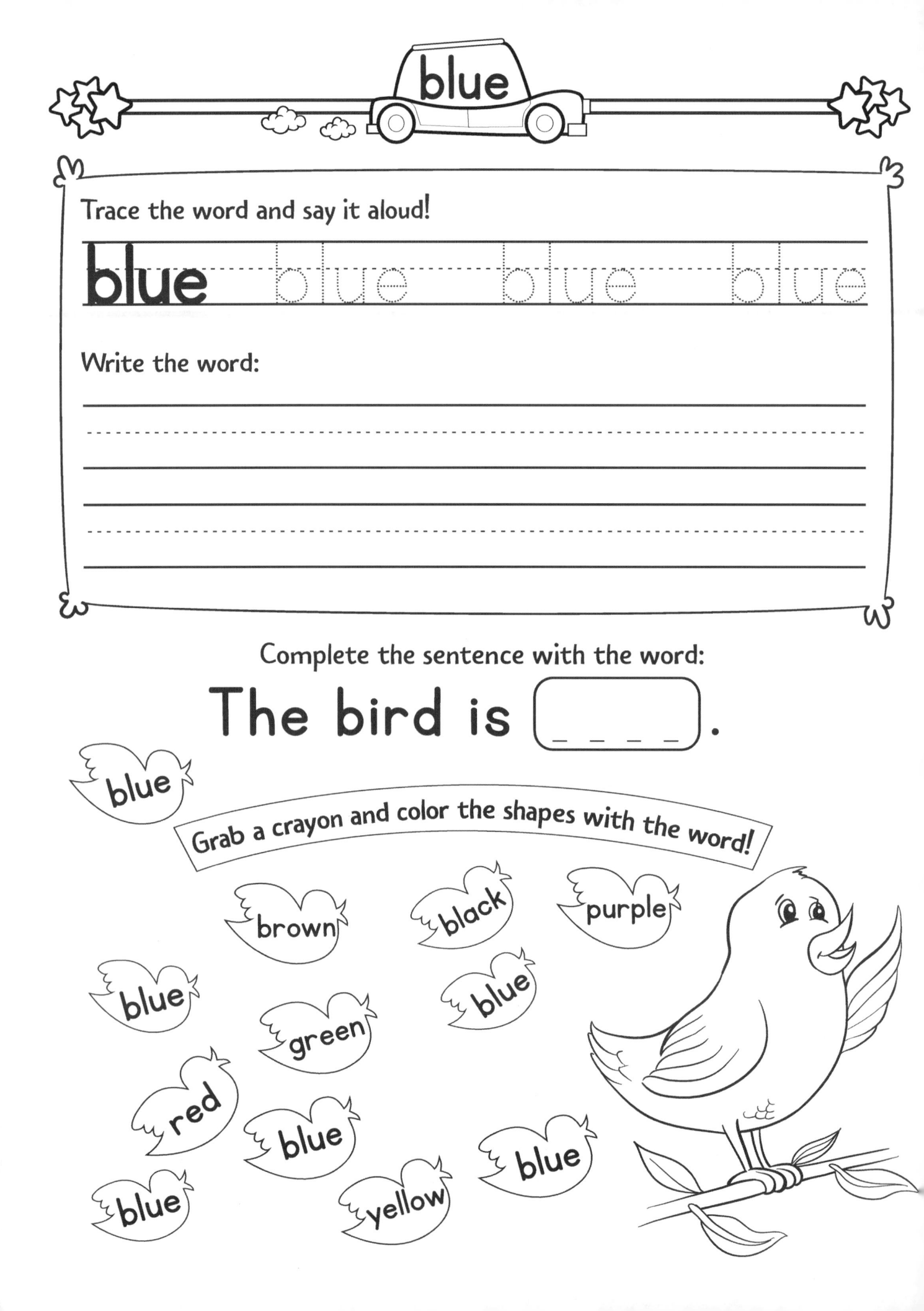

Trace the word and say it aloud!

blue blue blue blue

Write the word:

_____
_____
_____

Complete the sentence with the word:

The bird is [_ _ _ _].

Grab a crayon and color the shapes with the word!

blue
brown black purple
blue blue
green
red blue
blue yellow blue

brown

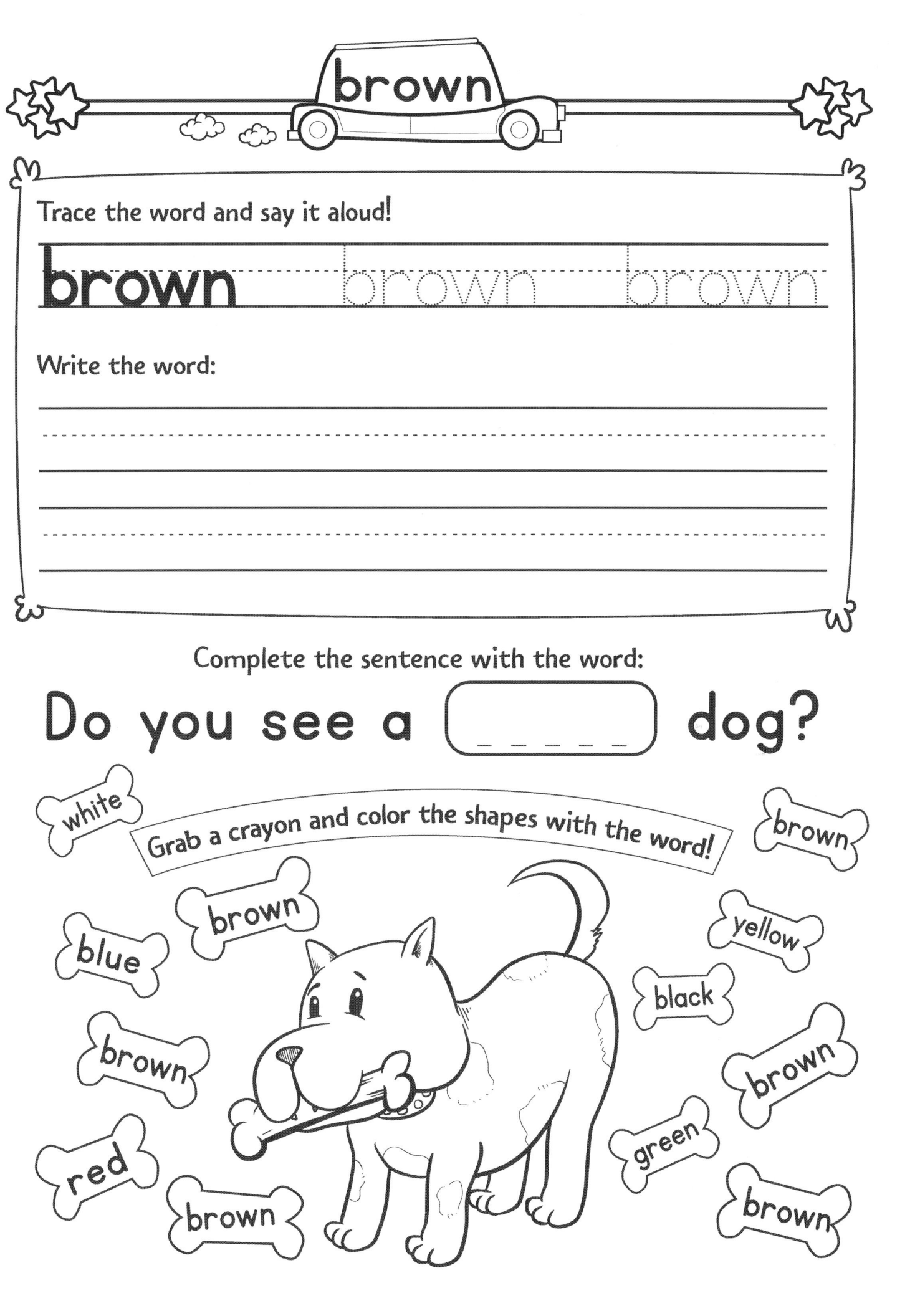

Trace the word and say it aloud!

brown   brown   brown

Write the word:

_____

Complete the sentence with the word:

Do you see a [_____] dog?

Grab a crayon and color the shapes with the word!

white   brown   blue   brown   red   brown   yellow   black   brown   green   brown

green

Trace the word and say it aloud!

green green green green

Write the word:

Complete the sentence with the word:

My bunny can play in the [_____] grass.

Grab a crayon and color the shapes with the word!

brown · green · green · yellow · green · red · blue · purple · green · green · black · green

orange

Trace the word and say it aloud!

orange orange orange

Write the word:

Complete the sentence with the word:

The fox has [_ _ _ _ _ _] fur.

Grab a crayon and color the shapes with the word!

yellow, orange, orange, black, orange, red, green, blue, orange, purple, orange, orange

pink

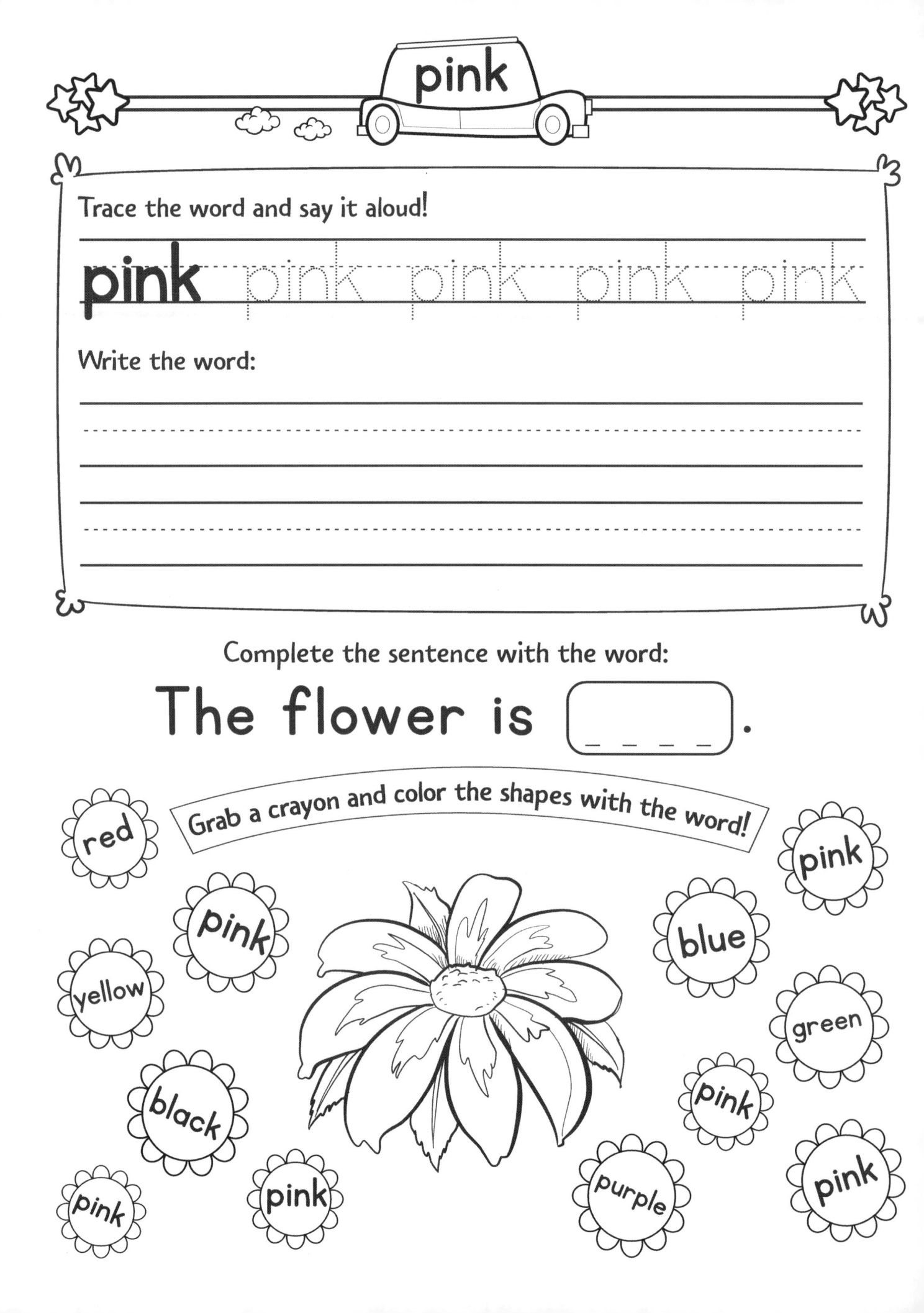

Trace the word and say it aloud!

pink pink pink pink pink

Write the word:

Complete the sentence with the word:

The flower is ☐ ☐ ☐ ☐ .

Grab a crayon and color the shapes with the word!

red pink pink blue yellow green pink black pink pink purple pink

purple

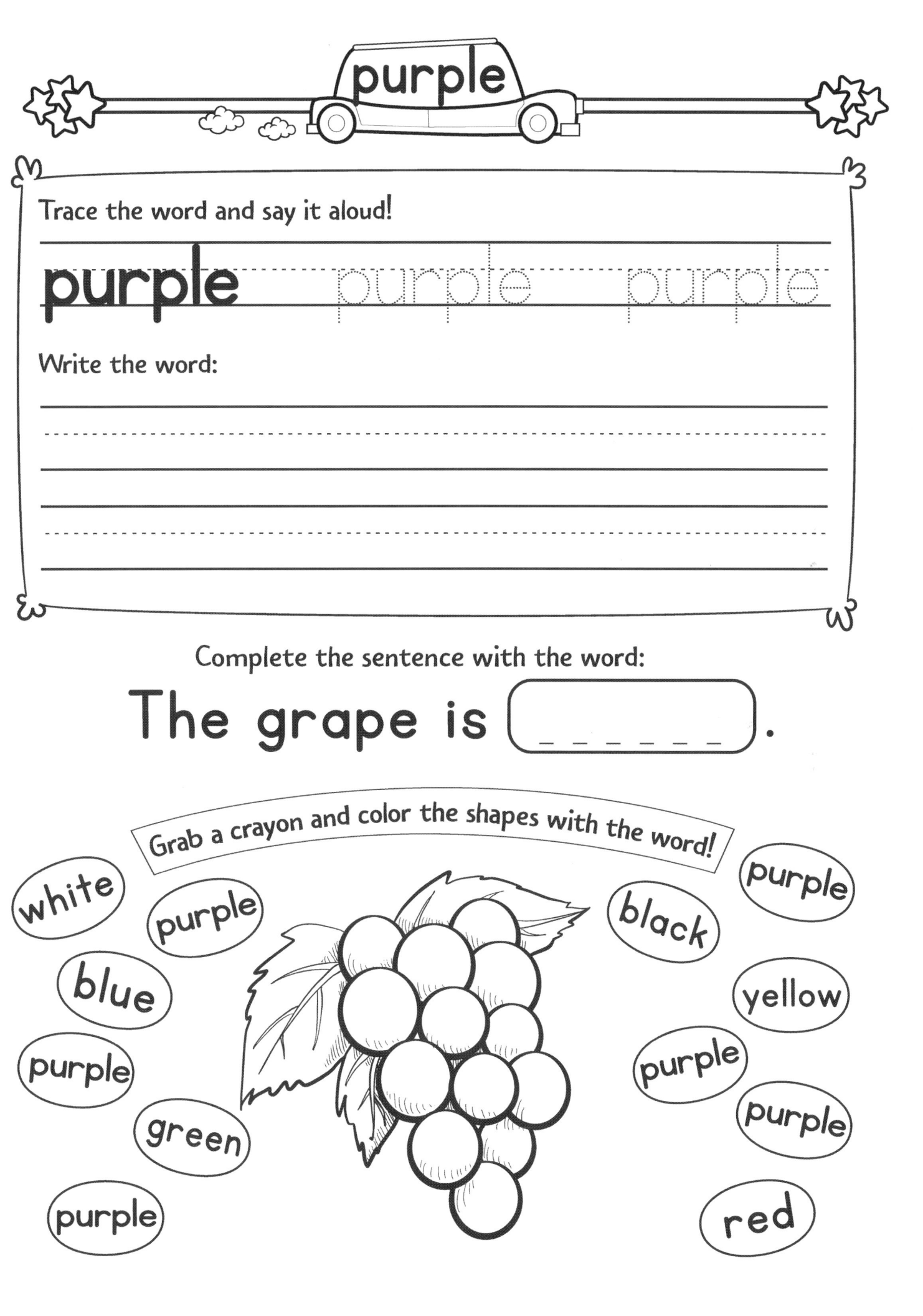

Trace the word and say it aloud!

purple purple purple

Write the word:

Complete the sentence with the word:

The grape is _____.

Grab a crayon and color the shapes with the word!

white purple black purple
blue yellow
purple purple
green purple
purple red

red

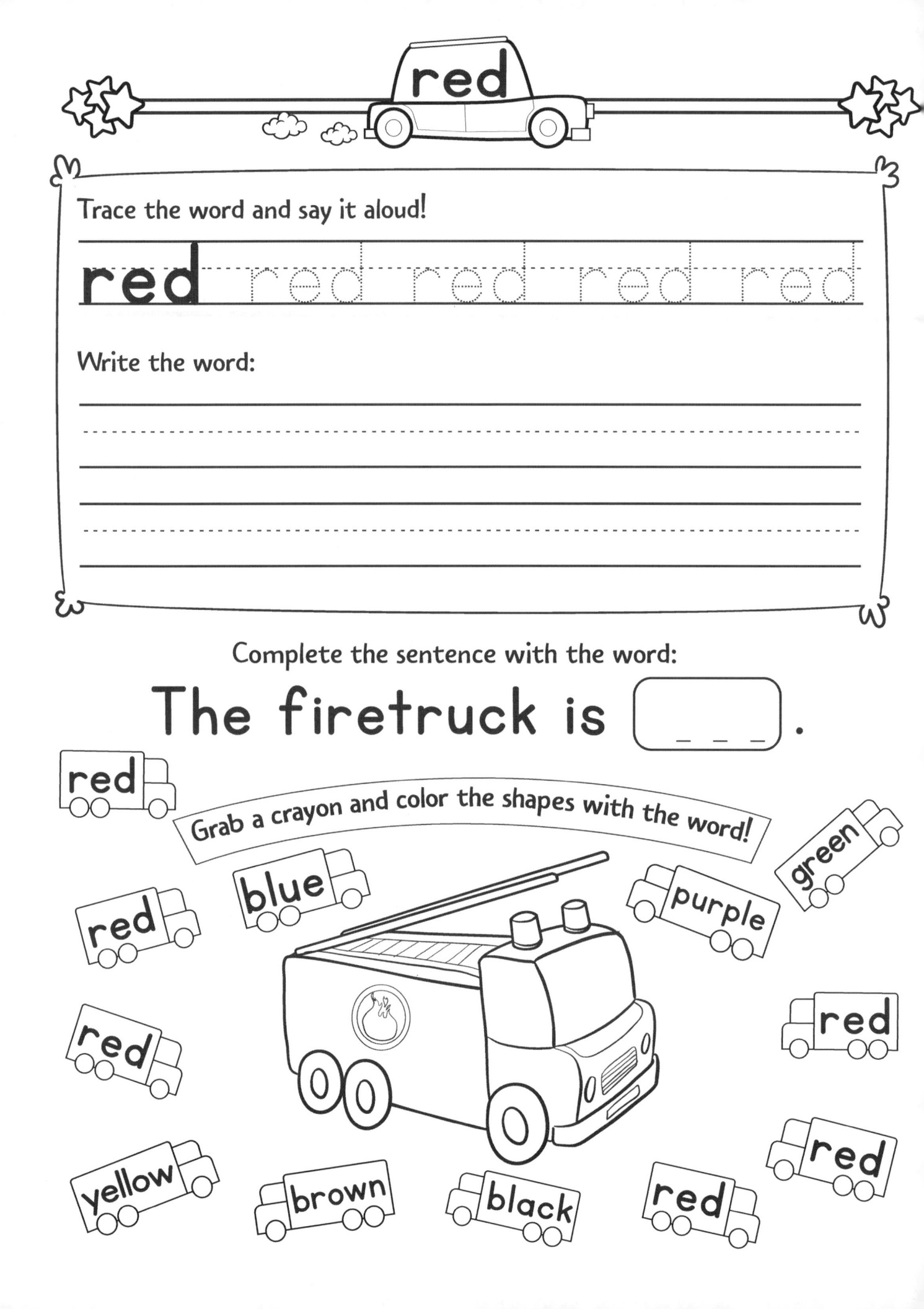

Trace the word and say it aloud!

red red red red red

Write the word:

Complete the sentence with the word:

The firetruck is ☐ ___ .

Grab a crayon and color the shapes with the word!

red • red • blue • purple • green • red • red • yellow • brown • black • red • red

white

Trace the word and say it aloud!

white white white white

Write the word:

Complete the sentence with the word:

The snowman was _____.

Grab a crayon and color the shapes with the word!

yellow

Trace the word and say it aloud!

yellow   yellow   yellow

Write the word:

Complete the sentence with the word:

The sun is _____.

Grab a crayon and color the shapes with the word!

black · blue · yellow · green · yellow · yellow · yellow · yellow · red · purple · yellow · brown

Trace the word and say it aloud!

a

Write the word:

Complete the sentence with the word:

I see ⬚ superhero.

Grab a crayon and color the shapes with the word!

a, all, a, at, am, a, are, a, and, a, an, a

all

Trace the word and say it aloud!

all all all all all all all

Write the word:

Complete the sentence with the word:

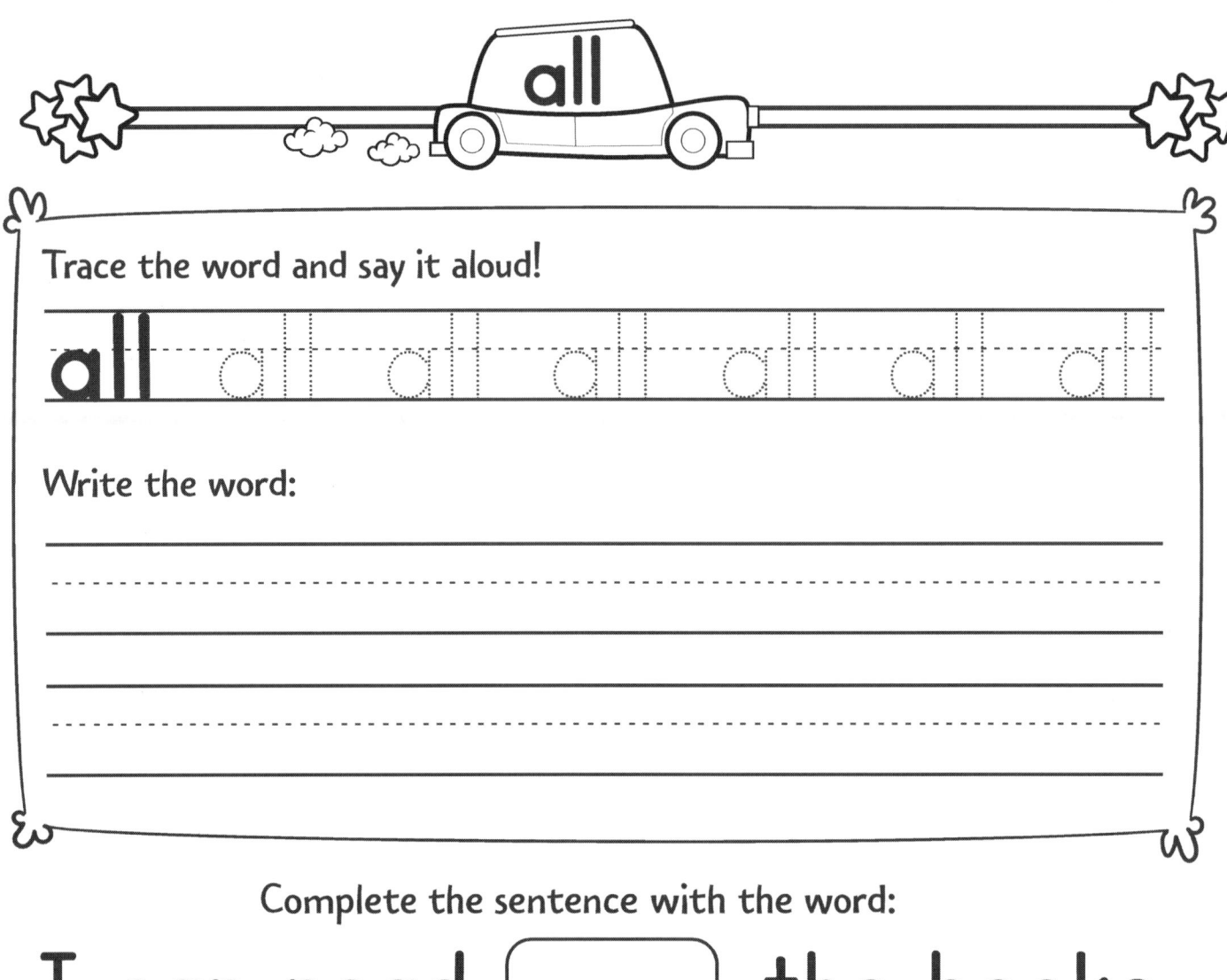

I can read [___] the books.

Grab a crayon and color the shapes with the word!

an · all · all · am · all · all · are · and · all · a · all · at

am

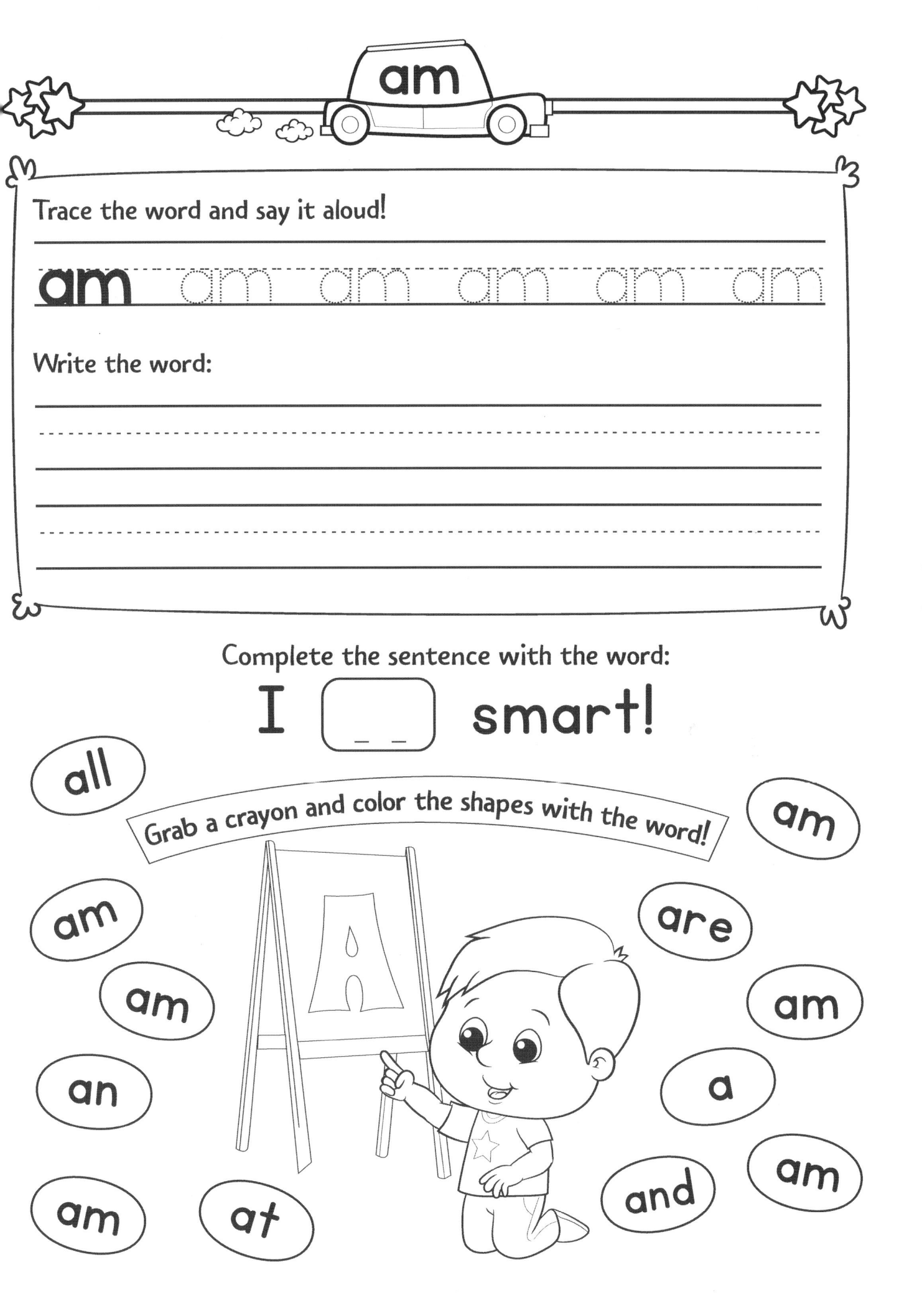

Trace the word and say it aloud!

am am am am am am

Write the word:

Complete the sentence with the word:

I [__] smart!

Grab a crayon and color the shapes with the word!

all   am   am   are   am   an   a   am   am   at   and

an

Trace the word and say it aloud!

an an an an an an an

Write the word:

Complete the sentence with the word:

Get [__] umbrella if it is going to rain.

Grab a crayon and color the shapes with the word!

and

Trace the word and say it aloud!

and and and and and

Write the word:

_____

_____

_____

_____

Complete the sentence with the word:

Dogs [___] cats like to play.

Grab a crayon and color the shapes with the word!

at • am • are • a • and • and • an • and • and • and • all • and

are

Trace the word and say it aloud!

are are are are are

Write the word:

Complete the sentence with the word:

Monsters [_ _ _] scary!

Grab a crayon and color the shapes with the word!

are · a · are · and · am · are · at · all · are · are · an

at

Trace the word and say it aloud!

at at at at at at at

Write the word:

Complete the sentence with the word:

You are good ▢ this!

Grab a crayon and color the shapes with the word!

at · all · one · am · a · at · at · away · an · at · at · at

ate

Trace the word and say it aloud!

ate   ate   ate   ate   ate

Write the word:

Complete the sentence with the word:

The dog ▯▯▯ the bone.

Grab a crayon and color the shapes with the word!

a   ate   ate   ate
ate
all   are
am   ate   ate
ate   an
and

away

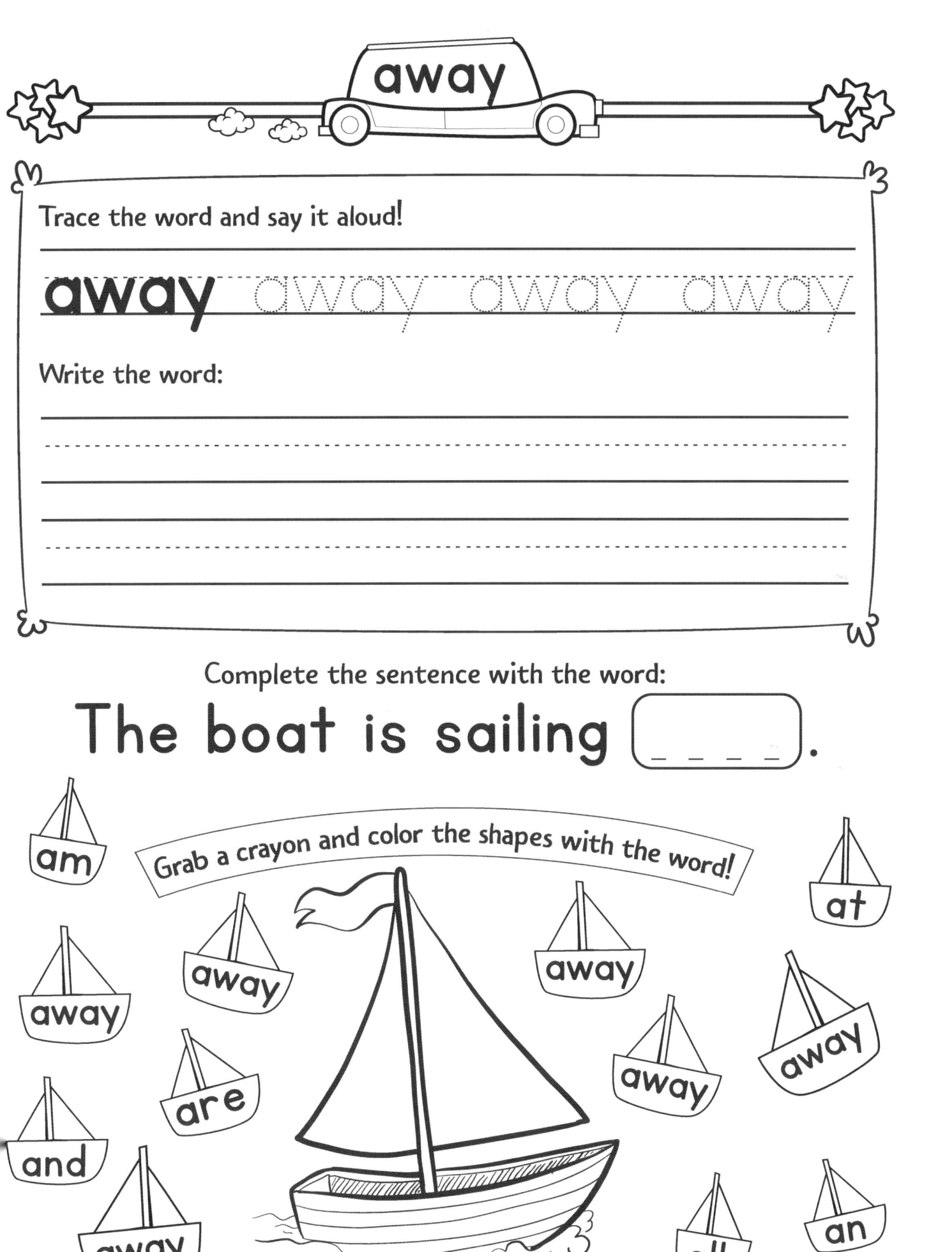

Trace the word and say it aloud!

away away away away

Write the word:

Complete the sentence with the word:

The boat is sailing ____.

Grab a crayon and color the shapes with the word!

am, at, away, away, away, away, are, away, and, all, an

be

Trace the word and say it aloud!

be be be be be be be

Write the word:

Complete the sentence with the word:

☐ the best you can!

Grab a crayon and color the shapes with the word!

be boy be be
but big
best be be box
be bad

big

Trace the word and say it aloud!

big big big big big big big

Write the word:

_____

_____

_____

Complete the sentence with the word:

The king lives in a [___] castle.

Grab a crayon and color the shapes with the word!

big but big be big boy

bus bad big big box big

but

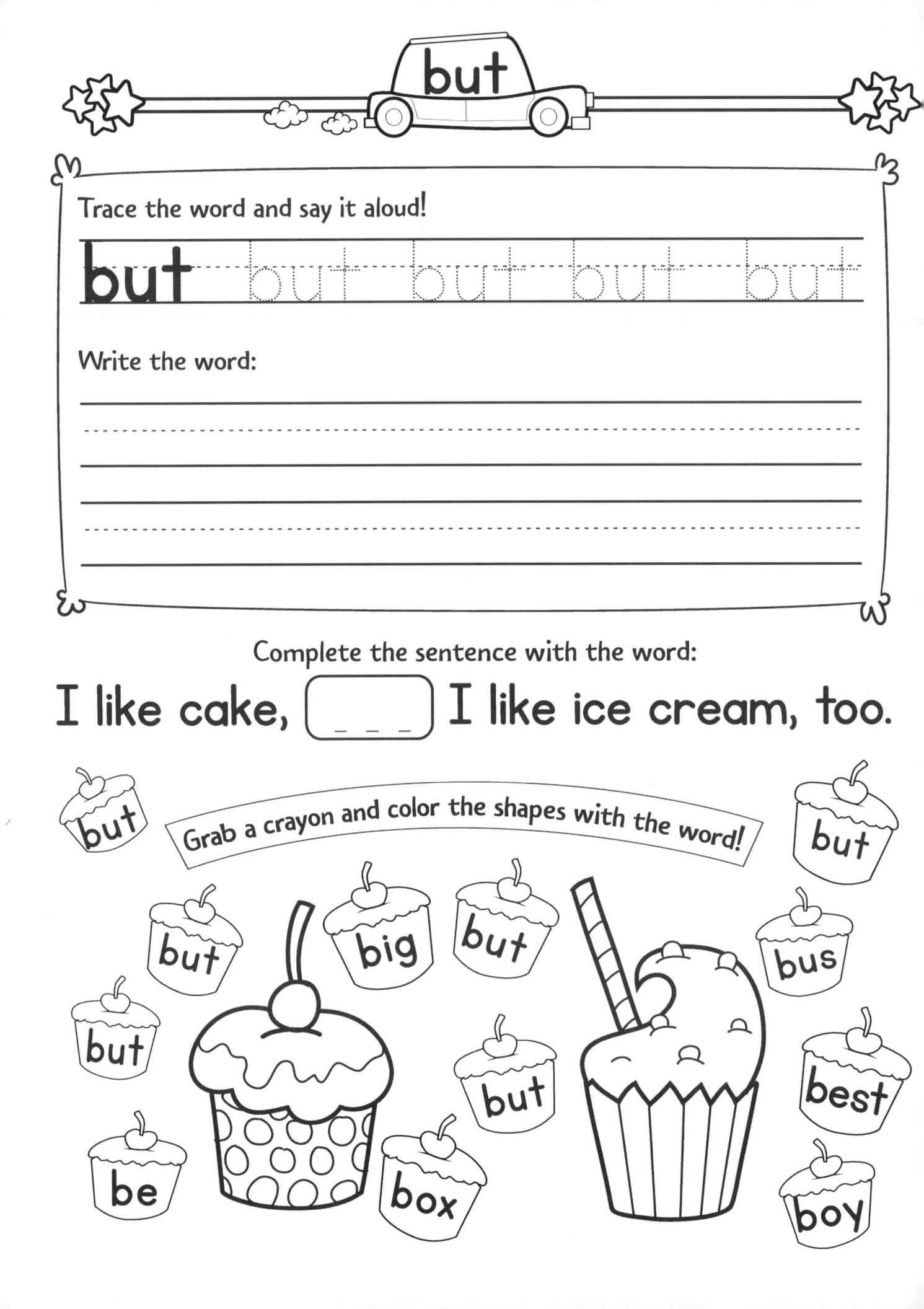

Trace the word and say it aloud!

but but but but but

Write the word:

Complete the sentence with the word:

I like cake, ⬜ I like ice cream, too.

Grab a crayon and color the shapes with the word!

but, but, big, but, but, but, bus, but, box, but, best, be, boy

came

Trace the word and say it aloud!

came came came came

Write the word:

Complete the sentence with the word:

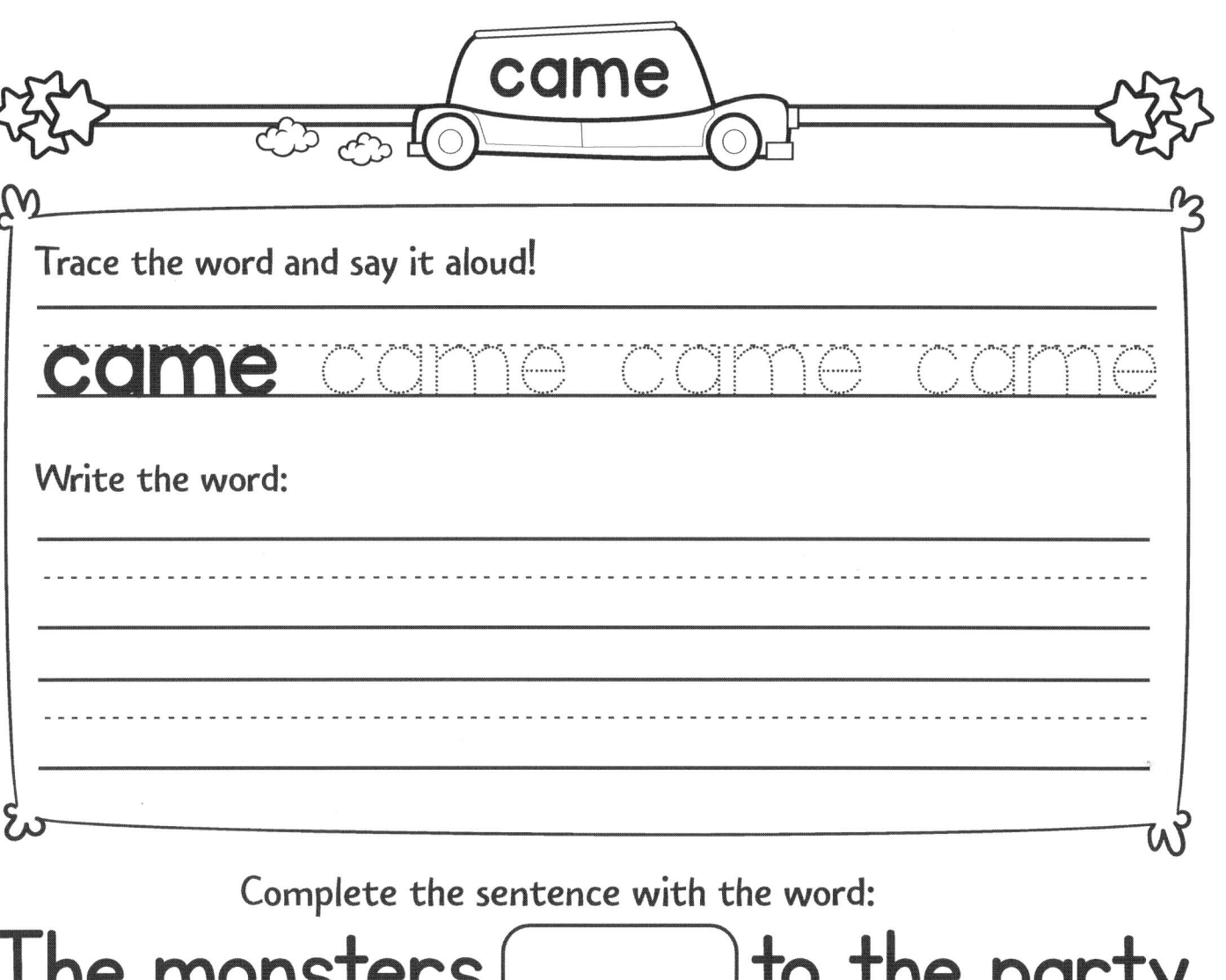

The monsters ☐ to the party.

Grab a crayon and color the shapes with the word!

car, came, cat, came, cup, came, came, cap, can, came, cut

come

Trace the word and say it aloud!

come come come come

Write the word:

Complete the sentence with the word:

Please [____] to our picnic.

Grab a crayon and color the shapes with the word!

come · can · come · cap · come · car · cup · come · cut · come · cat

can

Trace the word and say it aloud!

can can can can can

Write the word:

Complete the sentence with the word:

The truck [_ _ _] go fast.

Grab a crayon and color the shapes with the word!

can can cap car cut can cat can can came can cup

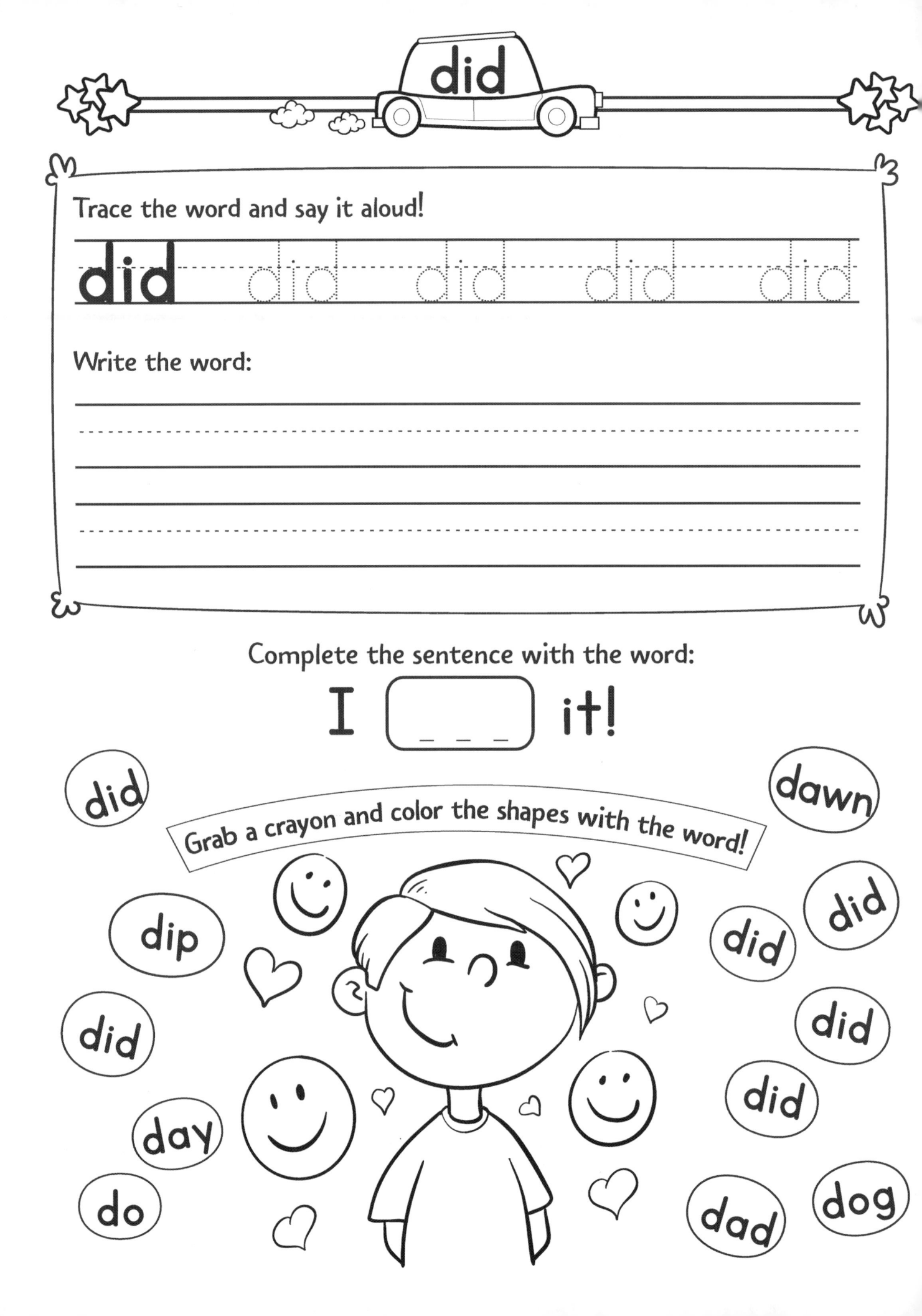

did

Trace the word and say it aloud!

did did did did did

Write the word:

_____

_____

_____

Complete the sentence with the word:

I [___] it!

Grab a crayon and color the shapes with the word!

did   dawn
dip   did   did
did   did
day   did
do   dad   dog

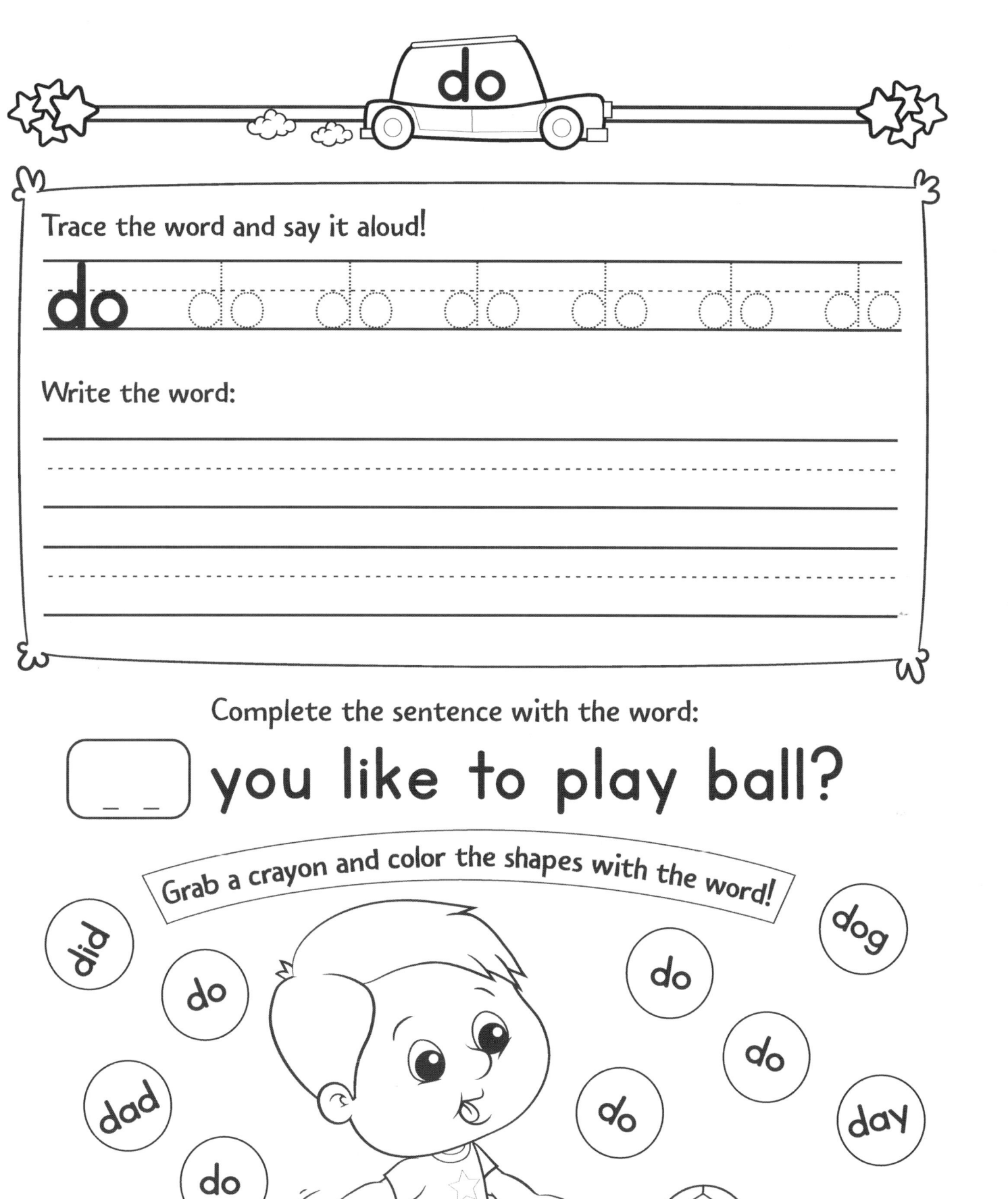

do

Trace the word and say it aloud!

do do do do do do do do

Write the word:

Complete the sentence with the word:

☐ you like to play ball?

Grab a crayon and color the shapes with the word!

did • do • dog • do • dad • do • day • do • dip • do • down

down

Trace the word and say it aloud!

down down down down

Write the word:

Complete the sentence with the word:

The fox runs [____] a hole.

Grab a crayon and color the shapes with the word!

dog down day did down dip down dad do down down down

eat

Trace the word and say it aloud!

eat eat eat eat eat

Write the word:

Complete the sentence with the word:

What do you like to ☐ ?

Grab a crayon and color the shapes with the word!

every · eat · eat · ear · eat · end · eat · even · egg · eat · eye · eat

find

Trace the word and say it aloud!

find find find find

Write the word:

Complete the sentence with the word:

Can you ____ a dinosaur?

Grab a crayon and color the shapes with the word!

fun fly find find find find find fan find for fix far

for

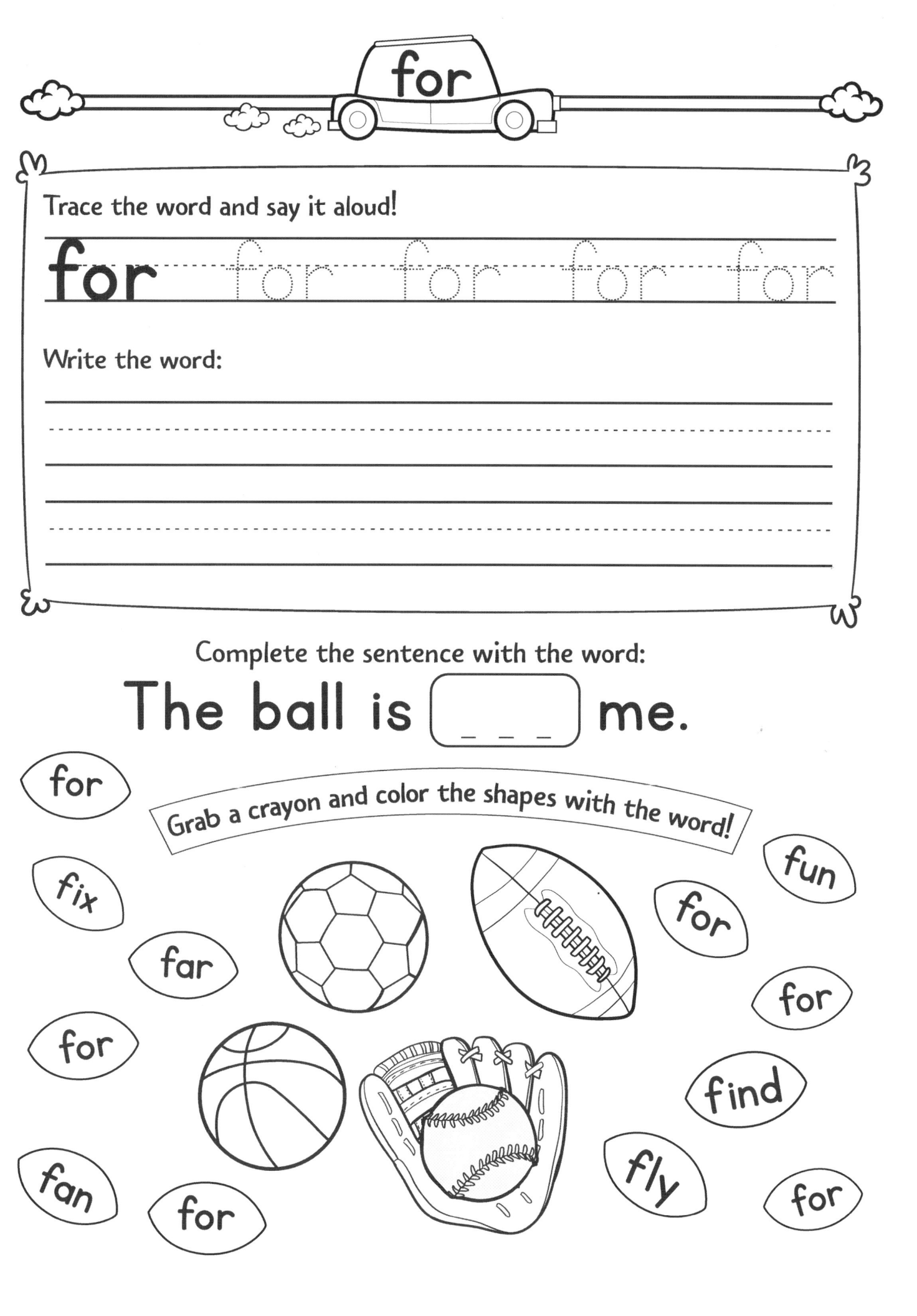

Trace the word and say it aloud!

for for for for for

Write the word:

Complete the sentence with the word:

The ball is ☐ me.

Grab a crayon and color the shapes with the word!

for fix far for fan for fun for for find fly for

get

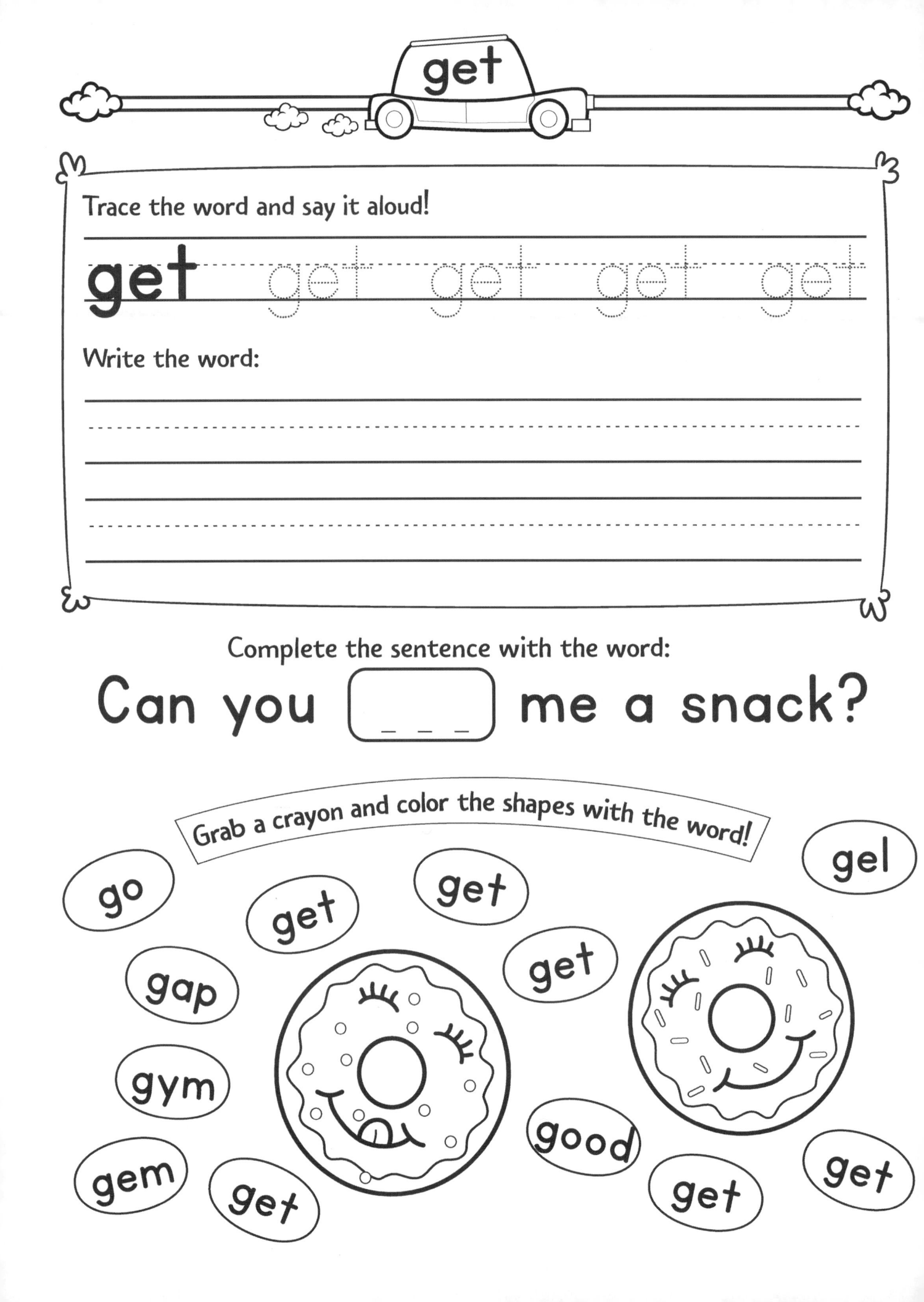

Trace the word and say it aloud!

get get get get get

Write the word:

Complete the sentence with the word:

Can you ☐ me a snack?

Grab a crayon and color the shapes with the word!

go   get   get   gel
gap   get
gym
gem   get   good   get   get

go

Trace the word and say it aloud!

go go go go go go go

Write the word:

Complete the sentence with the word:

The car can [__].

Grab a crayon and color the shapes with the word!

gel go gym go gap get go go go gem good go

good

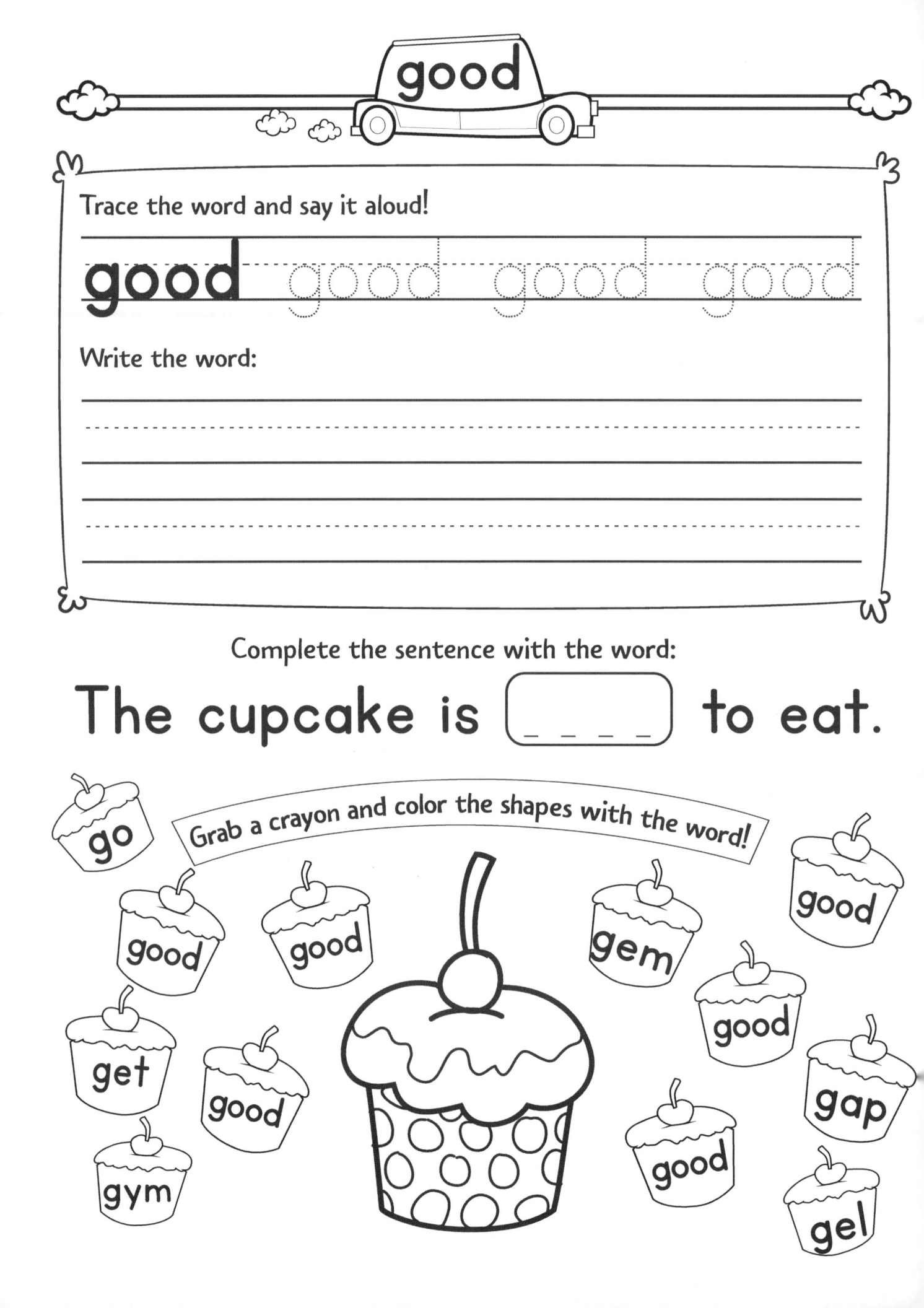

Trace the word and say it aloud!

good good good good

Write the word:

Complete the sentence with the word:

The cupcake is ____ to eat.

Grab a crayon and color the shapes with the word!

go
good
good
gem
good
get
good
good
gym
good
gap
gel

have

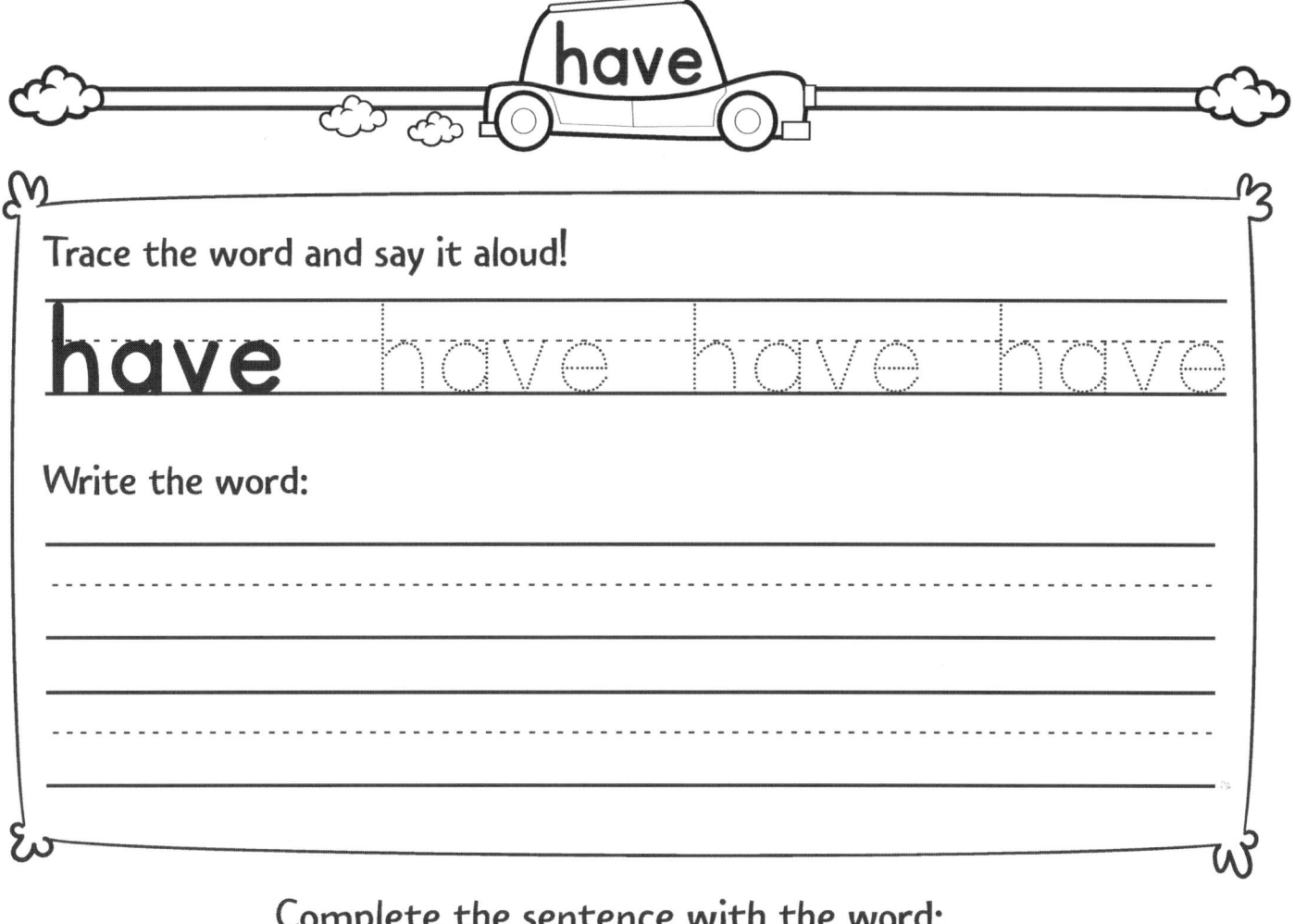

Trace the word and say it aloud!

have have have have

Write the word:

Complete the sentence with the word:

Can I [___] the toy?

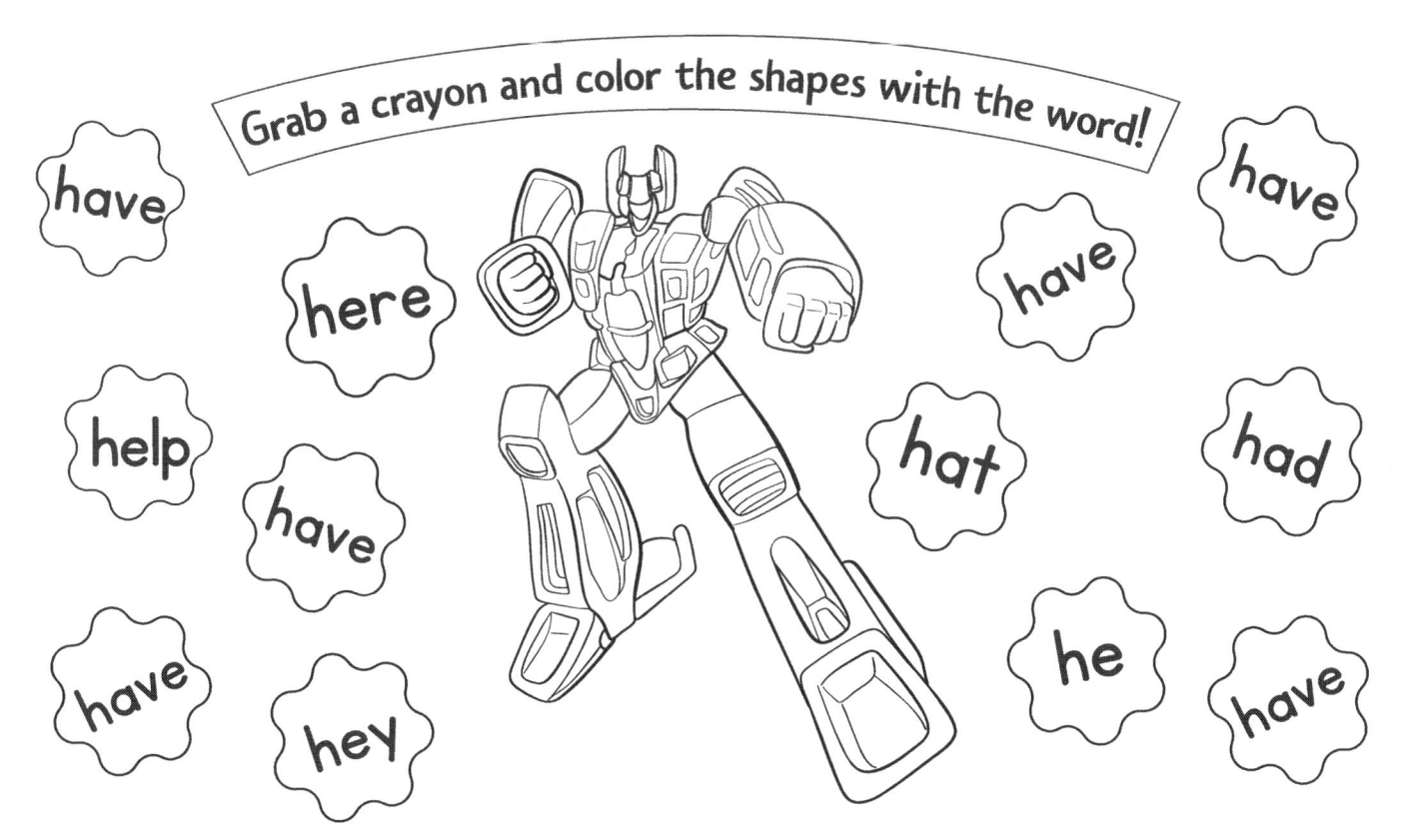

Grab a crayon and color the shapes with the word!

have · here · help · have · have · hey · have · hat · had · he · have

he

Trace the word and say it aloud!

he he he he he he he

Write the word:

Complete the sentence with the word:

☐ is my friend.

Grab a crayon and color the shapes with the word!

he • had • have • has • he • hat • here • hey • he • he

Trace the word and say it aloud!

help help help help help

Write the word:

Complete the sentence with the word:

I can [_ _ _ _] you.

Grab a crayon and color the shapes with the word!

have • help • here • help • had • hey • help • help • he • help • hat • help

four

Trace the word and say it aloud!

here here here here

Write the word:

Complete the sentence with the word:

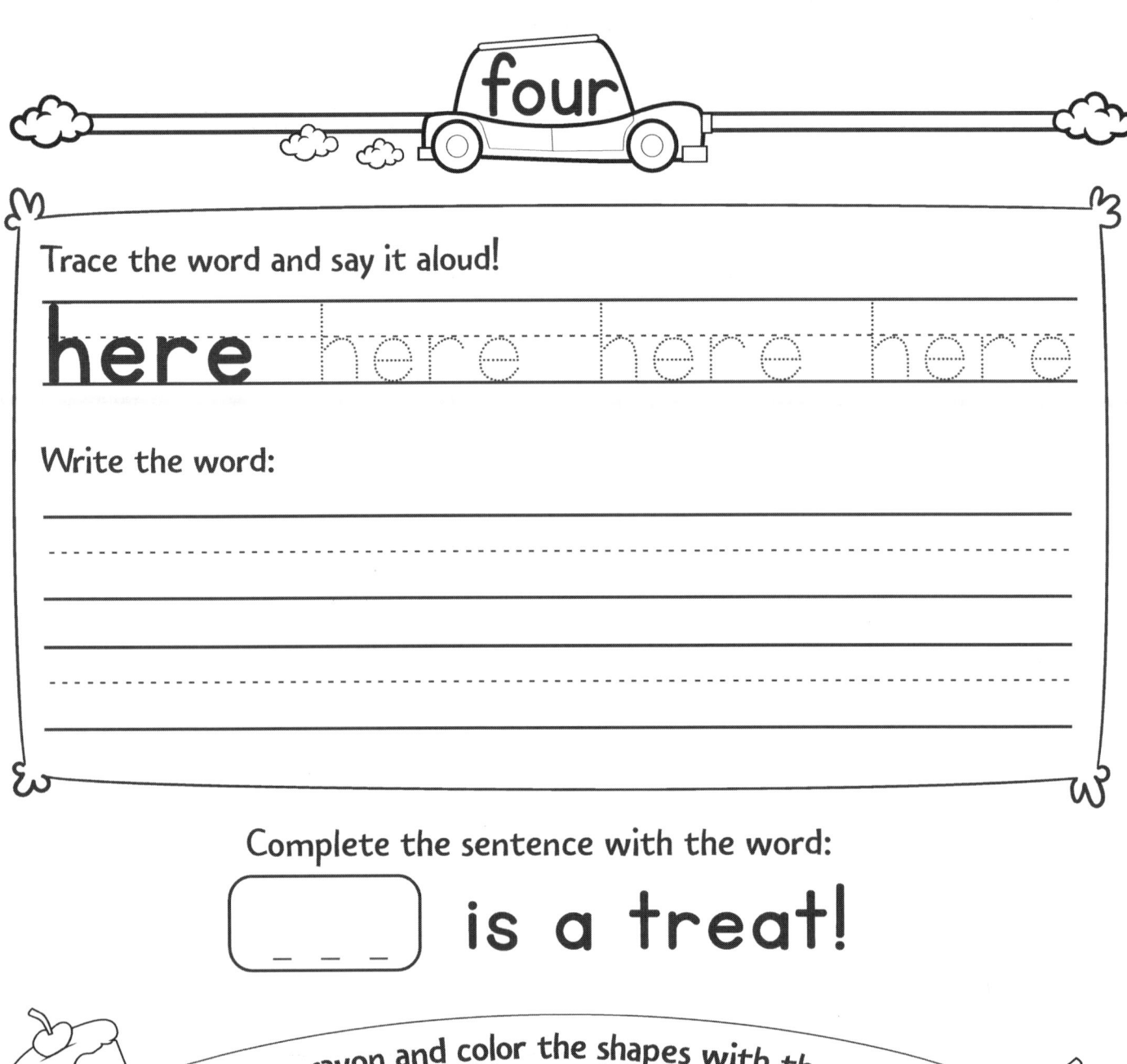

____ is a treat!

Grab a crayon and color the shapes with the word!

he has here help here
here have
hat here here he

Trace the word and say it aloud!

I

Write the word:

Complete the sentence with the word:

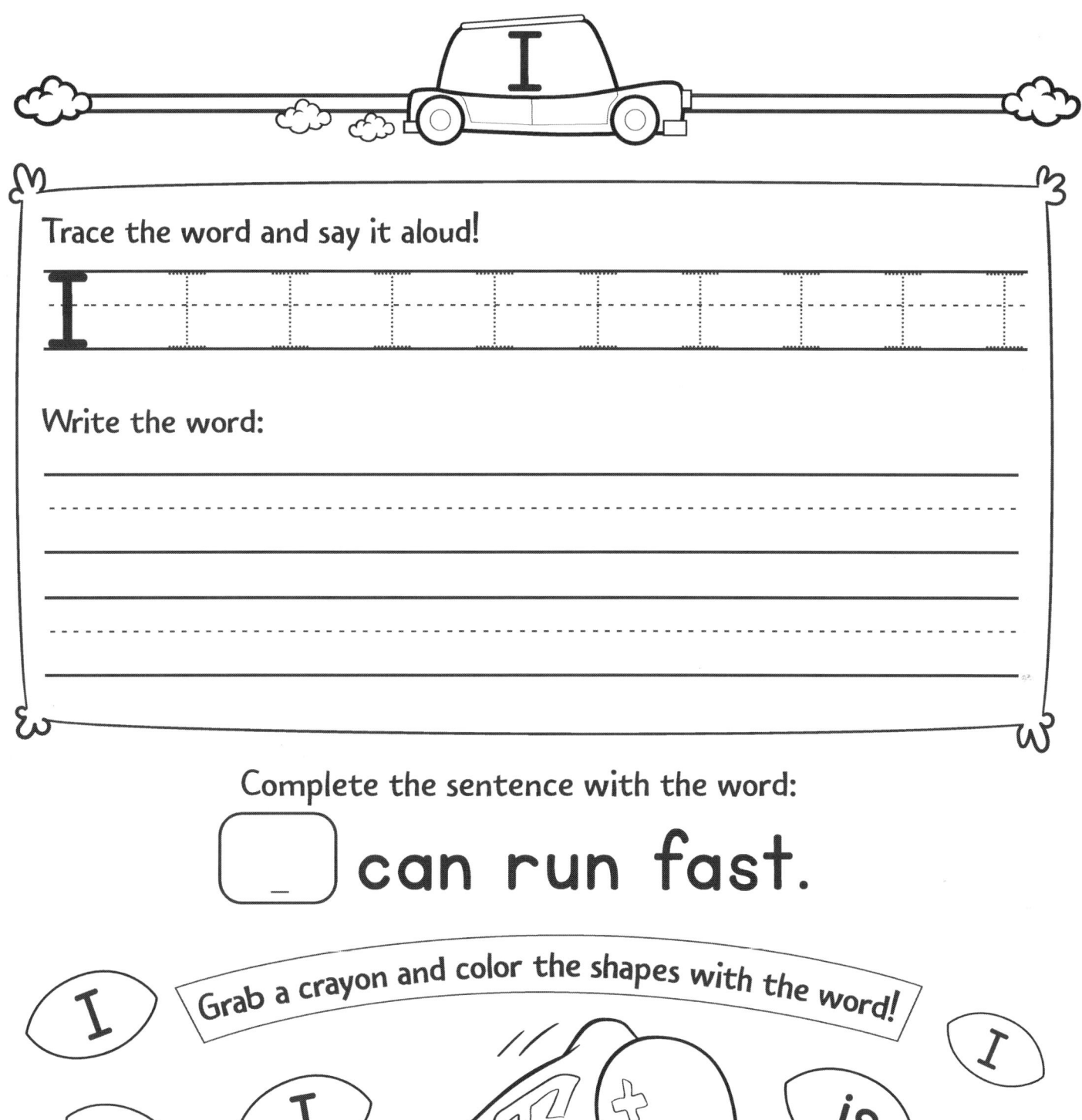

☐ can run fast.

Grab a crayon and color the shapes with the word!

I · it · I · is · I · if · I · ink · I · in · ice

in

Trace the word and say it aloud!

in   in   in   in   in   in   in

Write the word:

Complete the sentence with the word:

I can go ▢ the fort.

Grab a crayon and color the shapes with the word!

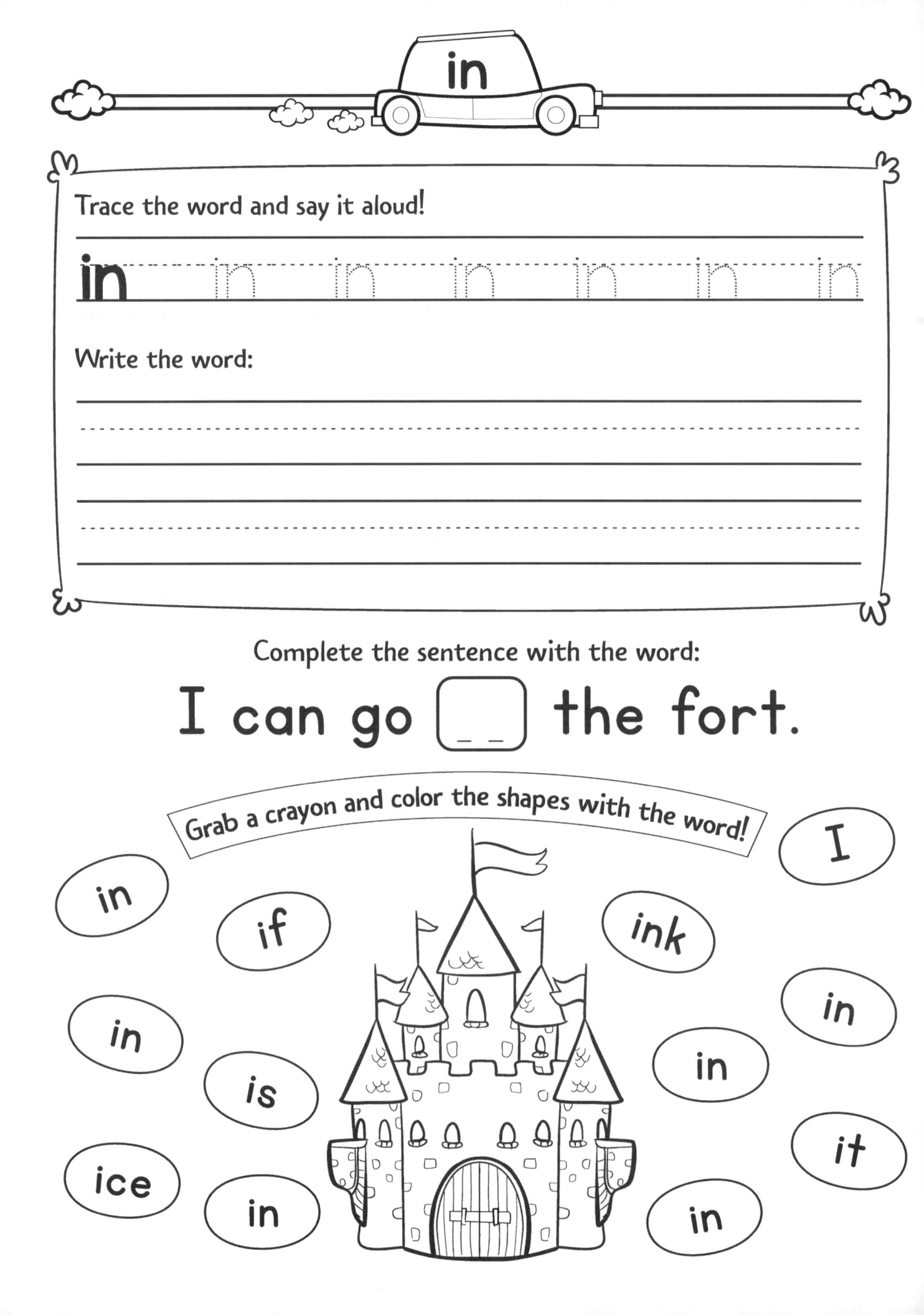

in   if   ink   I   in   in   in   in   is   it   ice   in   in

into

Trace the word and say it aloud!

into   into   into   into   into

Write the word:

Complete the sentence with the word:

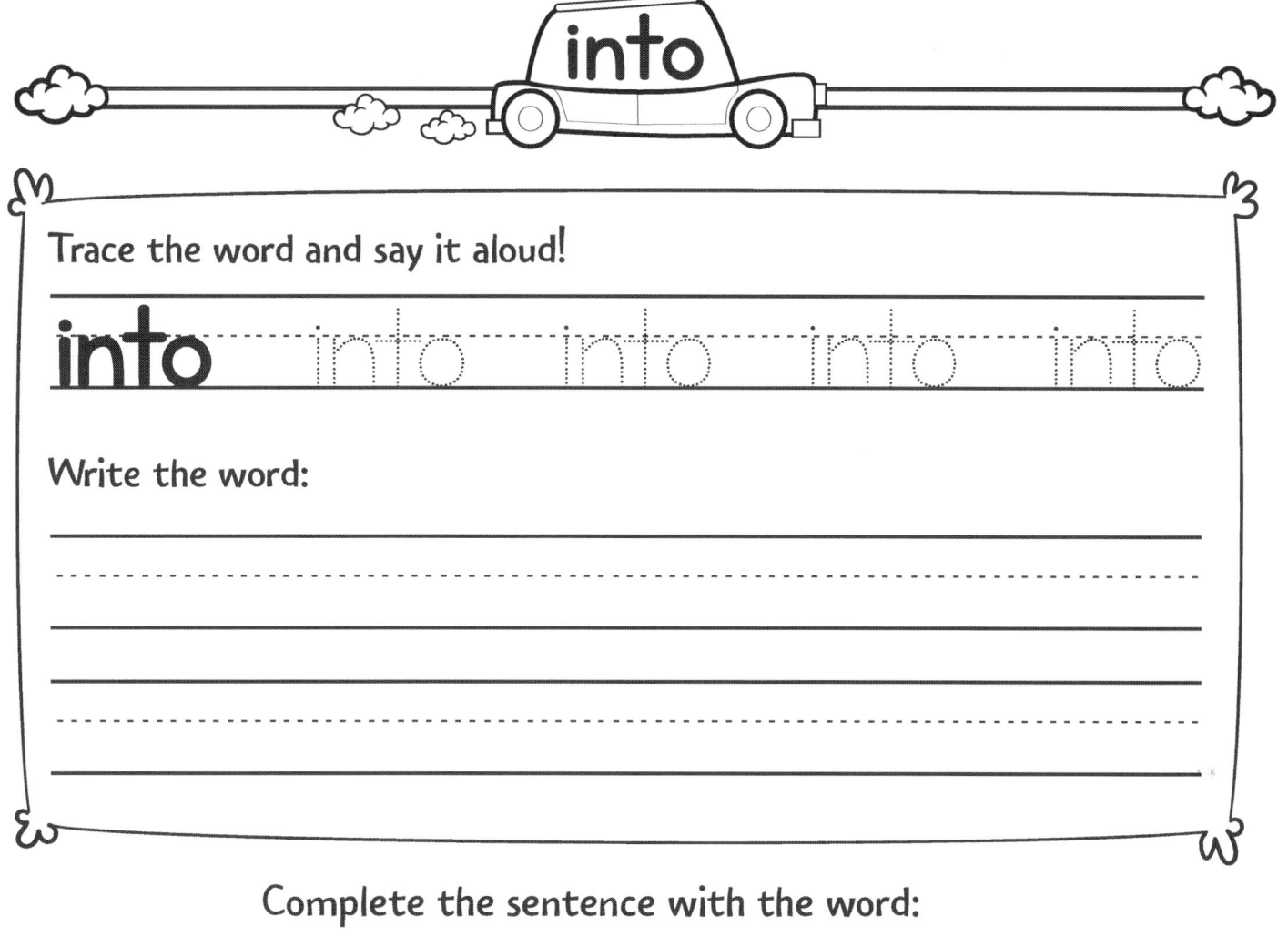

Put it [_ _ _ _] the dump truck.

Grab a crayon and color the shapes with the word!

I, into, in, it, into, into, if, into, into, ice, is, into

is

Trace the word and say it aloud!

is   is   is   is   is   is   is   is

Write the word:

Complete the sentence with the word:

The car ☐ slow.

Grab a crayon and color the shapes with the word!

I, is, is, is, in, ice, it, is, is, is, into, if

it

Trace the word and say it aloud!

it

Write the word:

Complete the sentence with the word:

[__] can fly far.

Grab a crayon and color the shapes with the word!

in   it   is   if   it   I   ice   it   it   it   into

jump

Trace the word and say it aloud!

jump jump jump jump

Write the word:

Complete the sentence with the word:

The boy can ____.

Grab a crayon and color the shapes with the word!

jump job jump jet jam jot jump jar joy jump jump jump

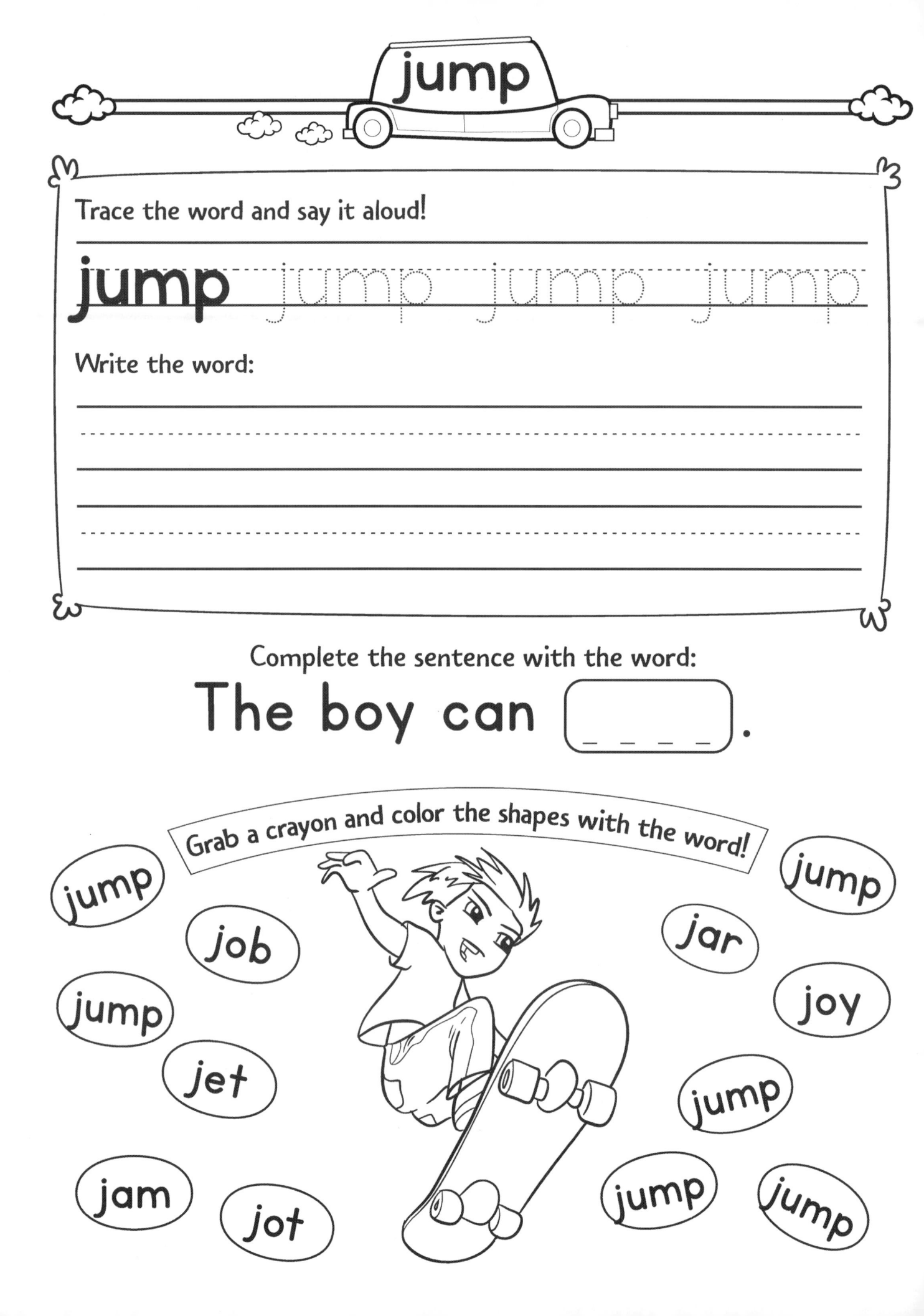

like

Trace the word and say it aloud!

like like like like like like

Write the word:

_____

Complete the sentence with the word:

I [_ _ _ _] you!

Grab a crayon and color the shapes with the word!

like · like · lid · little · like · leg · lot · like · lay · like · let

little

Trace the word and say it aloud!

little little little little

Write the word:

Complete the sentence with the word:

The bug is _____.

Grab a crayon and color the shapes with the word!

like little little little
leg   little
little   lid
lot let little lay

Trace the word and say it aloud!

look look look look look

Write the word:

Complete the sentence with the word:

I ▢ like a pirate.

Grab a crayon and color the shapes with the word!

look · lot · look · look · like · leg · little · let · look · lid · look · look

make

Trace the word and say it aloud!

make make make make

Write the word:

Complete the sentence with the word:

I can ☐ it go.

Grab a crayon and color the shapes with the word!

me
make
make
man
make may
make
map
mom
make
make
my

me

Trace the word and say it aloud!

me me me me me me

Write the word:

Complete the sentence with the word:

There is no one just like ▢!

mom

Grab a crayon and color the shapes with the word!

me
me
make
me
me
me
may
me
map
my
man

Trace the word and say it aloud!

my   my   my   my   my   my

Write the word:

Complete the sentence with the word:

☐ friend is happy.

Grab a crayon and color the shapes with the word!

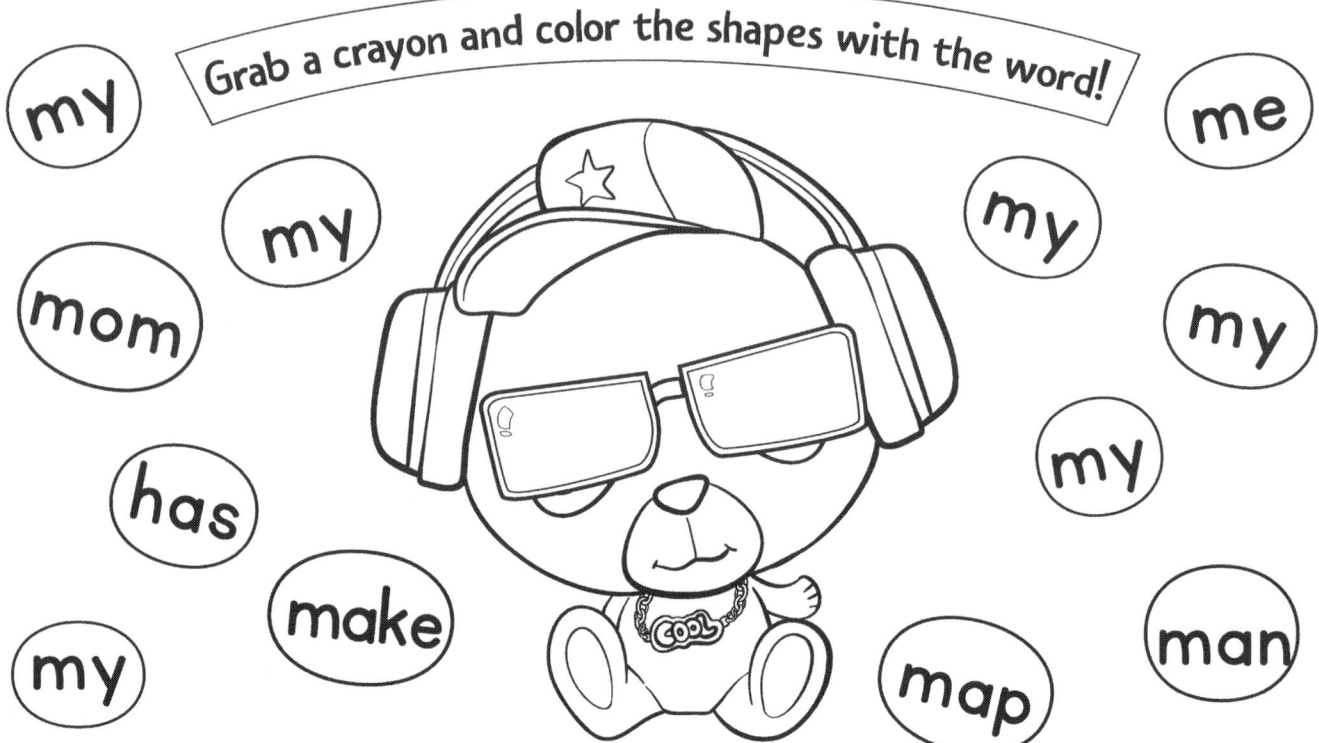

my my mom my has my make my me my my map man

new

Trace the word and say it aloud!

new new new new new

Write the word:

Complete the sentence with the word:

I want a ☐ bike.

Grab a crayon and color the shapes with the word!

nose — new — no — nap — new — net — new — now — not — new — new

no

Trace the word and say it aloud!

no no no no no no

Write the word:

Complete the sentence with the word:

☐, you can not have that toy.

Grab a crayon and color the shapes with the word!

no no new nose no net no not no no no now nap

not

Trace the word and say it aloud!

not not not not not not

Write the word:

Complete the sentence with the word:

That is [_ _ _] my dinosaur!

Grab a crayon and color the shapes with the word!

not   not   new   not   no   lot   nap   not   net   now   not

now

Trace the word and say it aloud!

now now now now now

Write the word:

Complete the sentence with the word:

Can I play with the truck ___?

Grab a crayon and color the shapes with the word!

no • now • now • new • nap • now • not • net • new • nose • now • now

on

Trace the word and say it aloud!

on on on on on on

Write the word:

Complete the sentence with the word:

I am ☐ the boat.

Grab a crayon and color the shapes with the word!

on
our
of
on
okay
on
out
on
on
one
on
or

our

Trace the word and say it aloud!

our our our our our

Write the word:

Complete the sentence with the word:

___ spaceship can fly high.

Grab a crayon and color the shapes with the word!

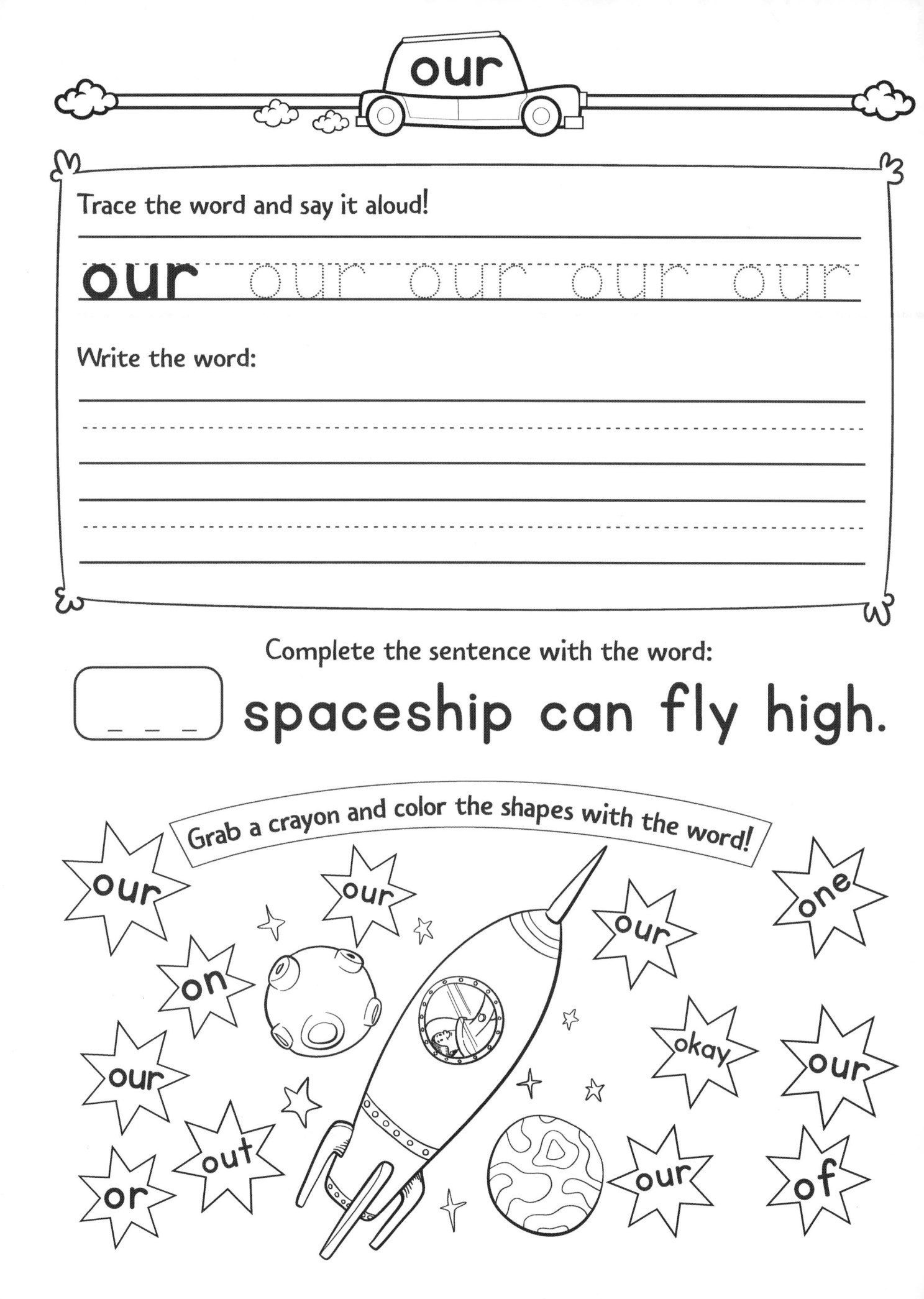

our · our · our · one
on · okay · our
our · our · of
or · out

out

Trace the word and say it aloud!

out out out out out

Write the word:

Complete the sentence with the word:

It is time to get ▢ of bed.

Grab a crayon and color the shapes with the word!

out on out out one our or okay out out of

play

Trace the word and say it aloud!

play   play   play   play

Write the word:

_____

_____

_____

Complete the sentence with the word:

Can the monster ☐, too?

Grab a crayon and color the shapes with the word!

pan play play play pot play pin pie play play put pet

please

Trace the word and say it aloud!

please   please   please

Write the word:

_____

_____

Complete the sentence with the word:

I would like some ice cream, _____ .

Grab a crayon and color the shapes with the word!

- please
- pan
- pie
- please
- pin
- please
- pot
- please
- please
- put
- pet
- please

pretty

Trace the word and say it aloud!

pretty   pretty   pretty

Write the word:

Complete the sentence with the word:

My mom's flowers are _____.

Grab a crayon and color the shapes with the word!

put, pin, pretty, pan, pretty, pretty, pie, pretty, pretty, pot, pet

ran

Trace the word and say it aloud!

ran ran ran ran ran

Write the word:

Complete the sentence with the word:

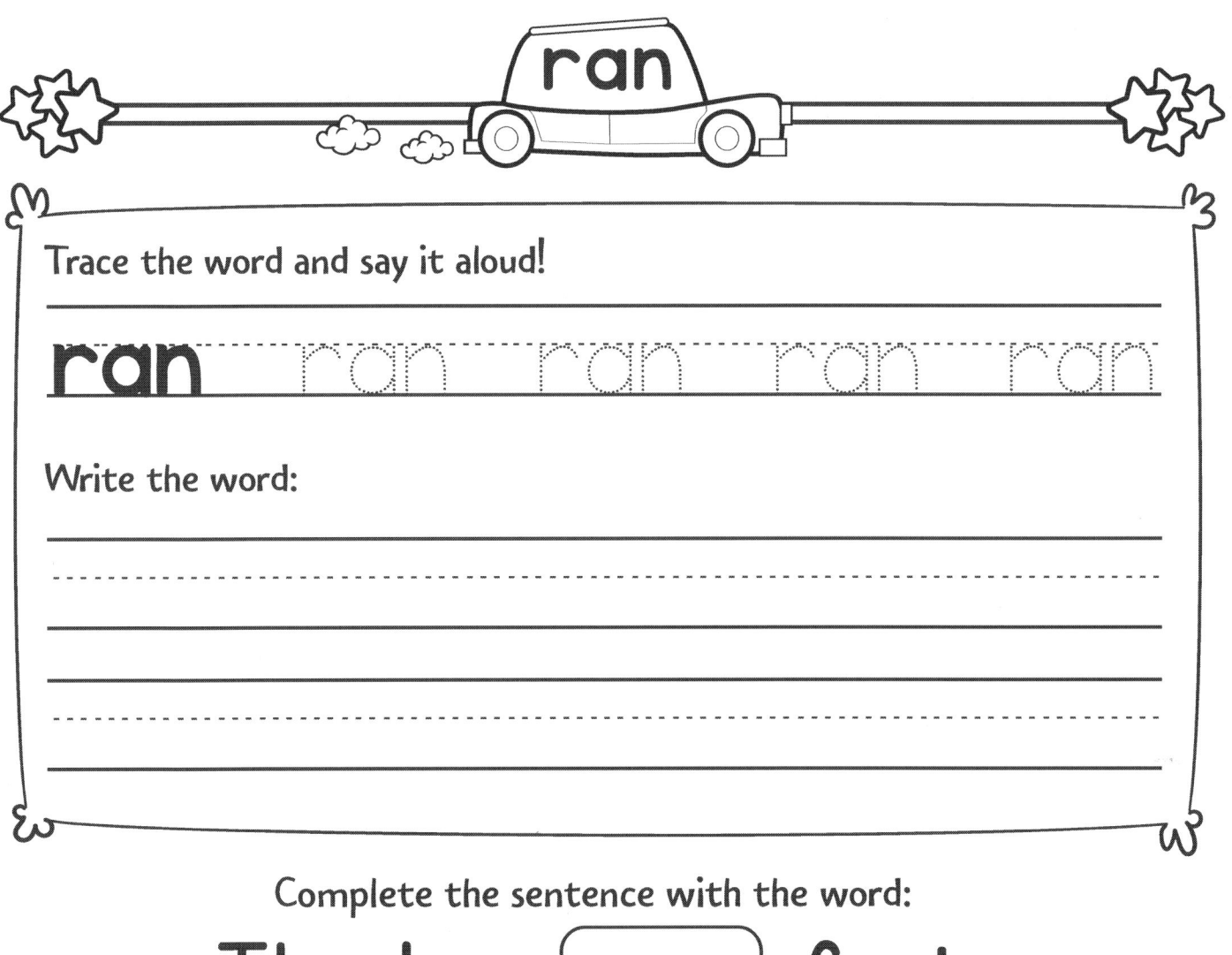

The boy ▢ fast.

Grab a crayon and color the shapes with the word!

ran   rid   ran   ran
ram   red
row   ran   rod
ran   ran
                 rig

ride

Trace the word and say it aloud!

ride ride ride ride ride

Write the word:

_____

_____

Complete the sentence with the word:

I [___] in the monster truck.

Grab a crayon and color the shapes with the word!

rid · ride · ran · ride · ride · ram · row · ride · red · ride · rod · ride

run

Trace the word and say it aloud!

run run run run run

Write the word:

Complete the sentence with the word:

The dog likes to ___ .

Grab a crayon and color the shapes with the word!

run ran ride run run ram rod red run rid run

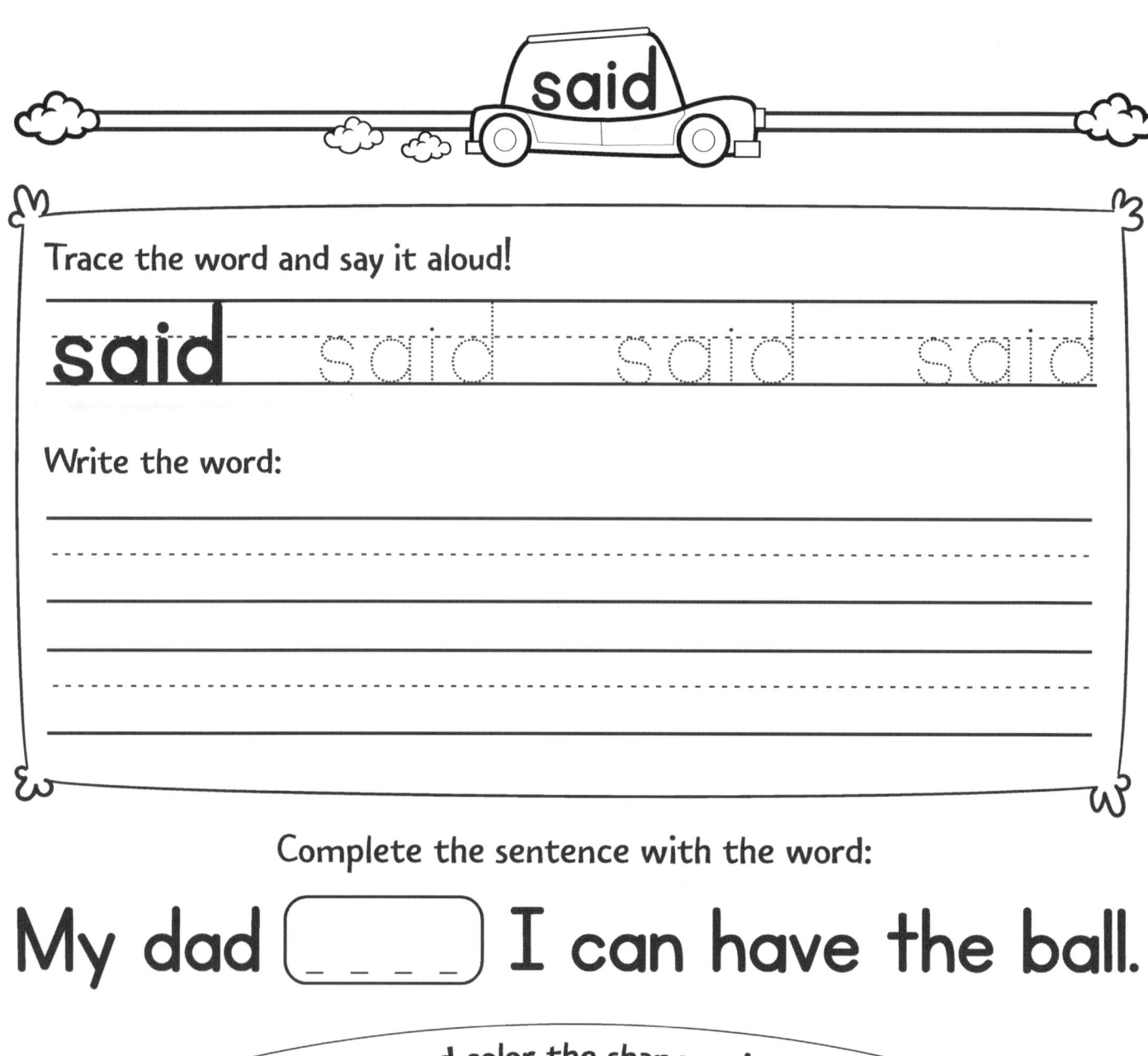

said

Trace the word and say it aloud!

said   said   said   said

Write the word:

Complete the sentence with the word:

My dad [___] I can have the ball.

Grab a crayon and color the shapes with the word!

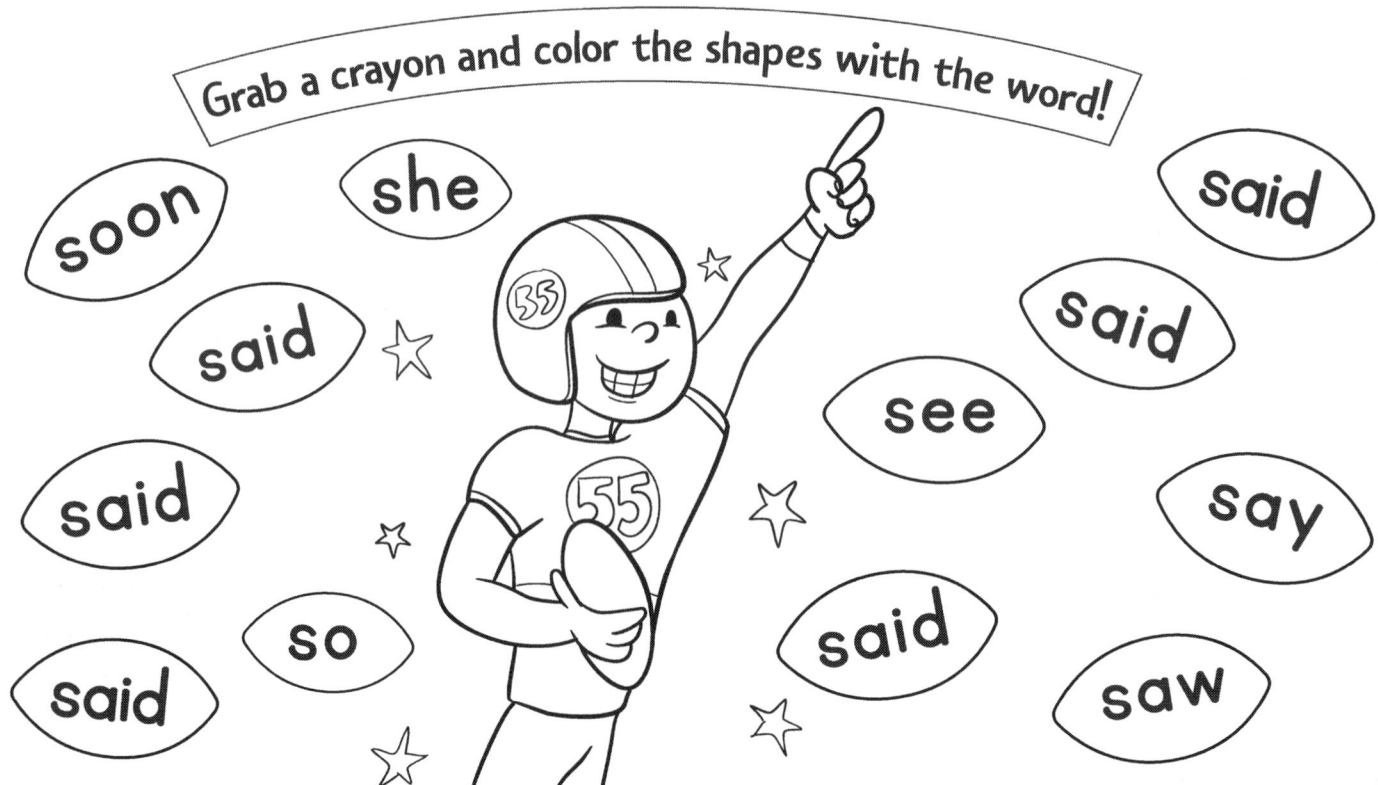

soon, she, said, said, said, said, see, said, say, so, said, said, saw

saw

Trace the word and say it aloud!

saw saw saw saw saw

Write the word:

Complete the sentence with the word:

He ▢▢▢ the airplane.

Grab a crayon and color the shapes with the word!

saw, see, saw, said, saw, say, soon, she, saw, so, saw

say

Trace the word and say it aloud!

say say say say say

Write the word:

Complete the sentence with the word:

What did he ☐___.

Grab a crayon and color the shapes with the word!

see · so · say · saw · say · soon · say · say · said · say · she

see

Trace the word and say it aloud!

see   see   see   see   see

Write the word:

Complete the sentence with the word:

I can [_ _ _] the stars.

Grab a crayon and color the shapes with the word!

see, saw, see, she, see, say, soon, so, see, see, said

she

Trace the word and say it aloud!

she she she she she

Write the word:

Complete the sentence with the word:

☐ likes to run with me.

Grab a crayon and color the shapes with the word!

say · she · she · see · she · soon · said · so · she · she · she · saw so

Trace the word and say it aloud!

so so so so so so so

Write the word:

Complete the sentence with the word:

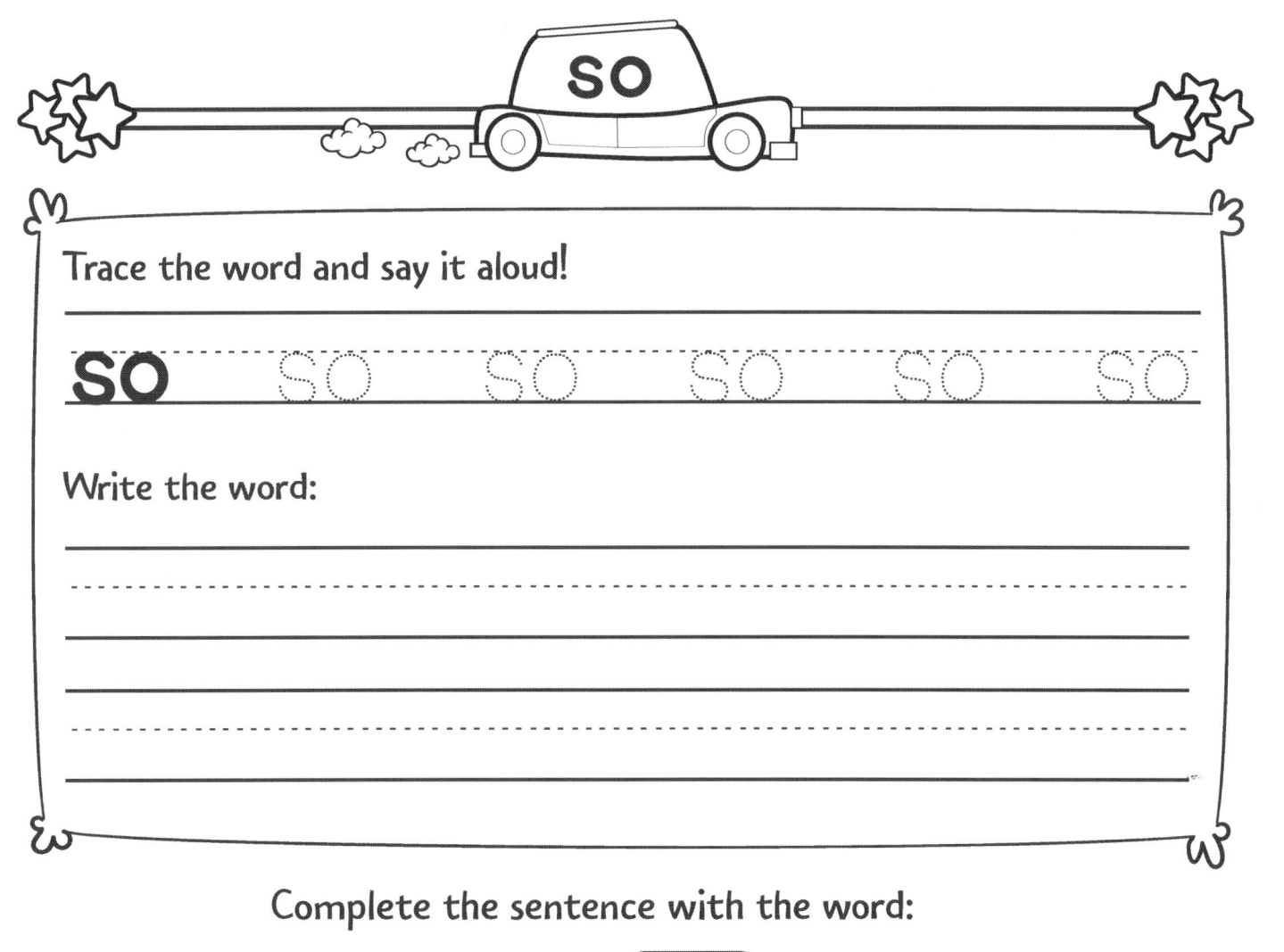

My bike is broken, [ ] I can not ride.

Grab a crayon and color the shapes with the word!

so · said · so · so · say · so · she · see · so · soon · saw · so

soon

Trace the word and say it aloud!

soon soon soon soon

Write the word:

Complete the sentence with the word:

We can go to the party ☐ .

Grab a crayon and color the shapes with the word!

soon · soon · soon · see · saw · said · she · soon · soon · say · so · soon

that

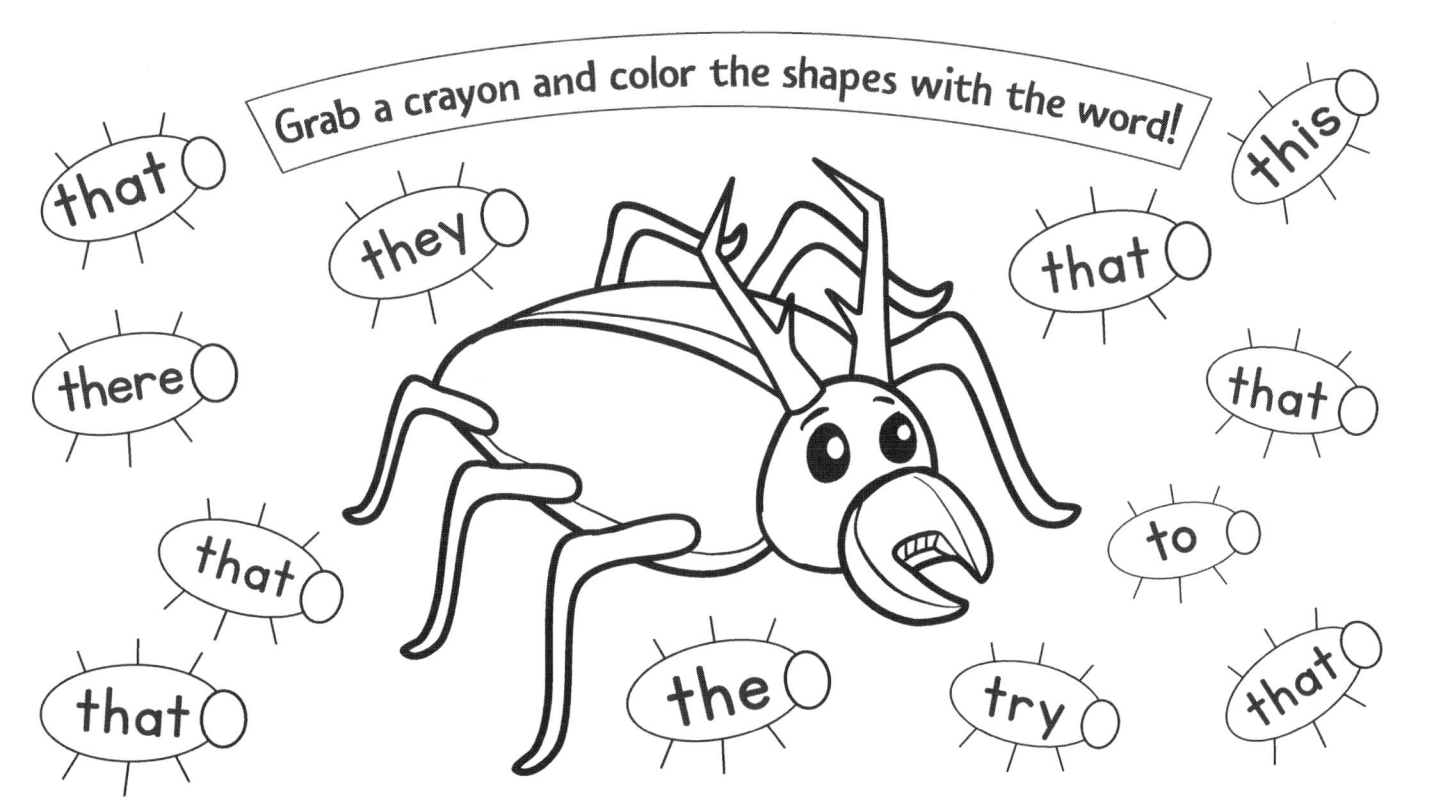

Trace the word and say it aloud!

that   that   that   that

Write the word:

Complete the sentence with the word:

☐ bug has six legs.

Grab a crayon and color the shapes with the word!

that they this that there that that to that the try that

the

Trace the word and say it aloud!

the   the   the   the   the

Write the word:

_____

_____

_____

Complete the sentence with the word:

[___] bulldozer can dig dirt.

Grab a crayon and color the shapes with the word!

to, the, this, the, the, try, that, the, there, they, the, the

there

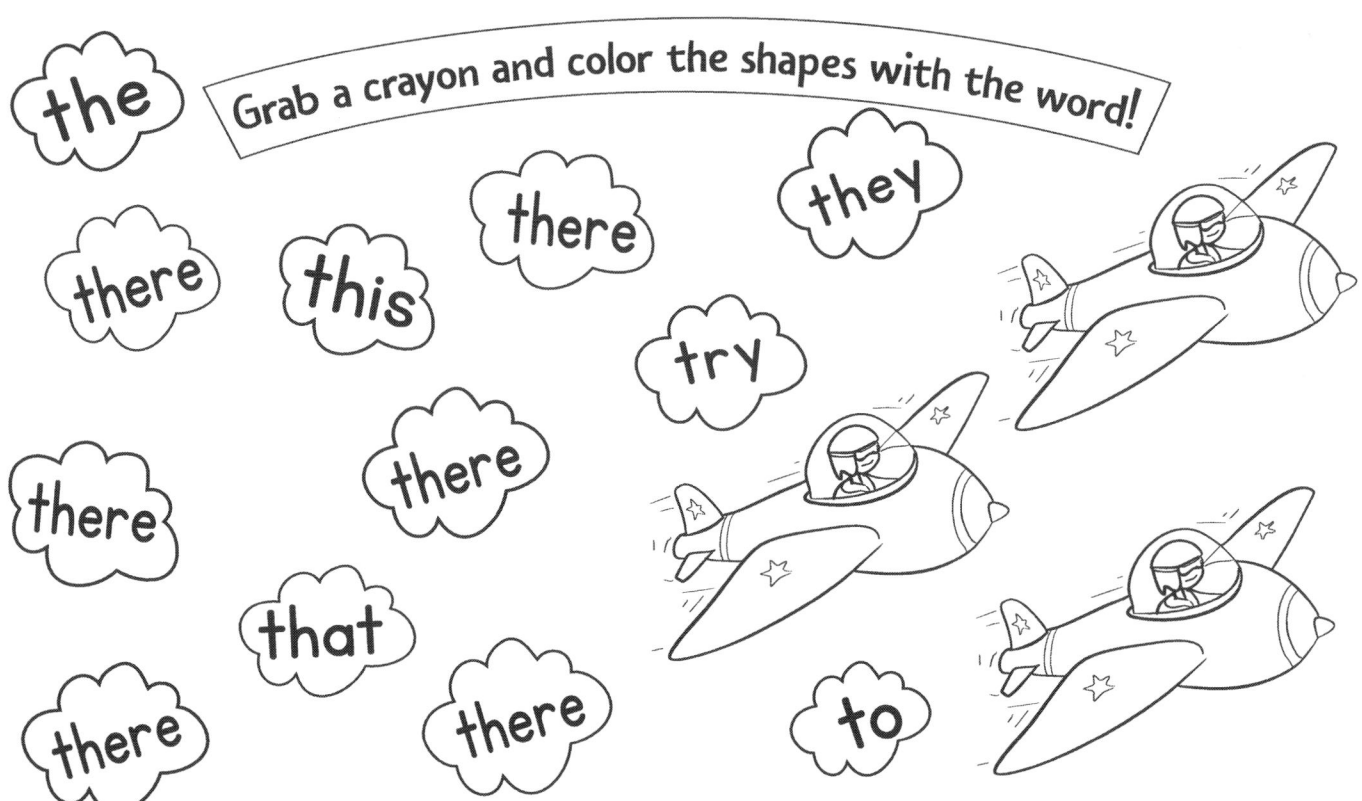

Trace the word and say it aloud!

there there there there

Write the word:

Complete the sentence with the word:

☐ are three airplanes in the sky.

Grab a crayon and color the shapes with the word!

the, there, this, there, they, try, there, that, there, there, to

they

Trace the word and say it aloud!

they they they they

Write the word:

Complete the sentence with the word:

☐ can jump.

Grab a crayon and color the shapes with the word!

the this they they there they that try they they to

this

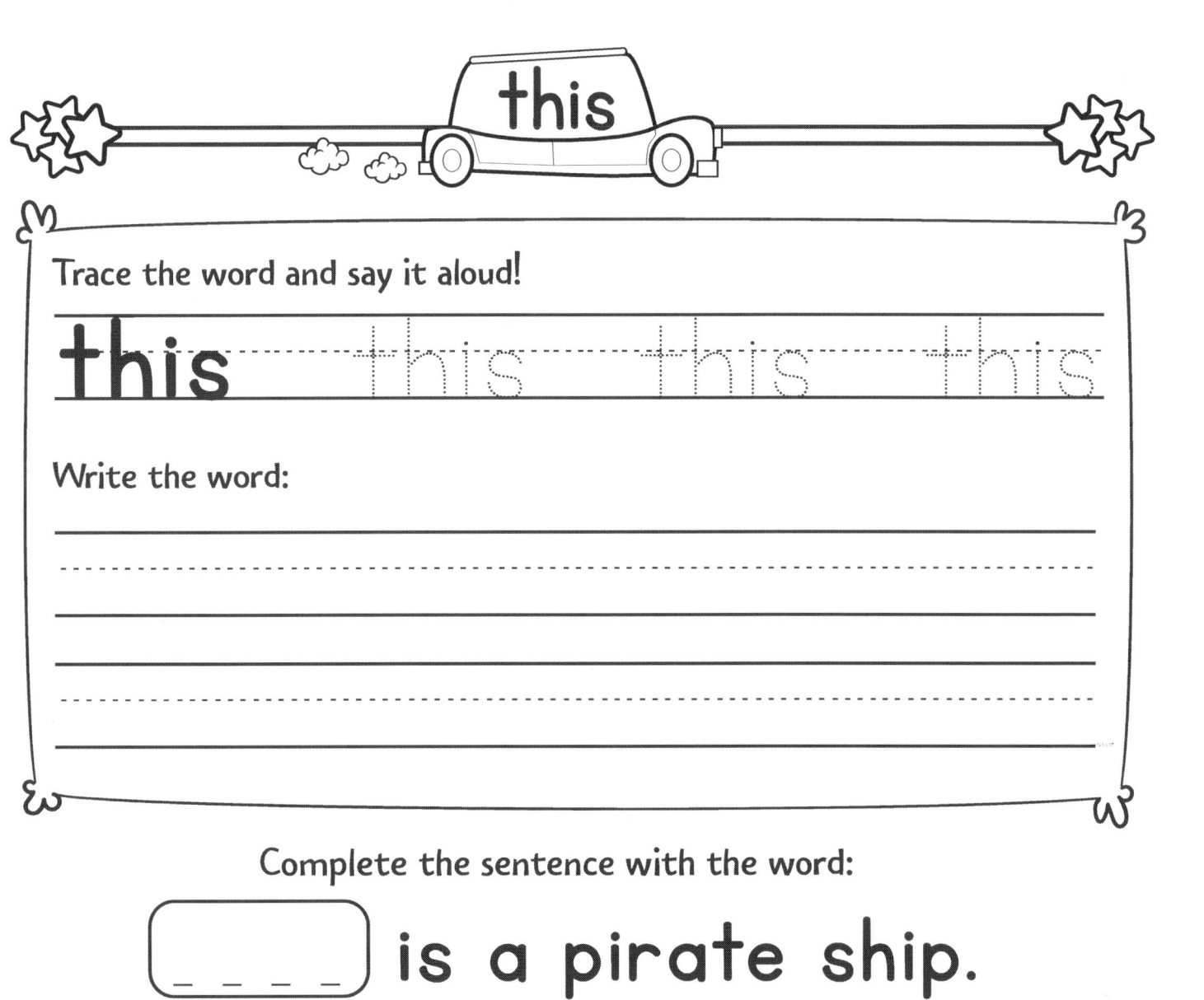

Trace the word and say it aloud!

this this this this

Write the word:

Complete the sentence with the word:

____ is a pirate ship.

Grab a crayon and color the shapes with the word!

this · there · this · that · this · the · they · this · this · to · try

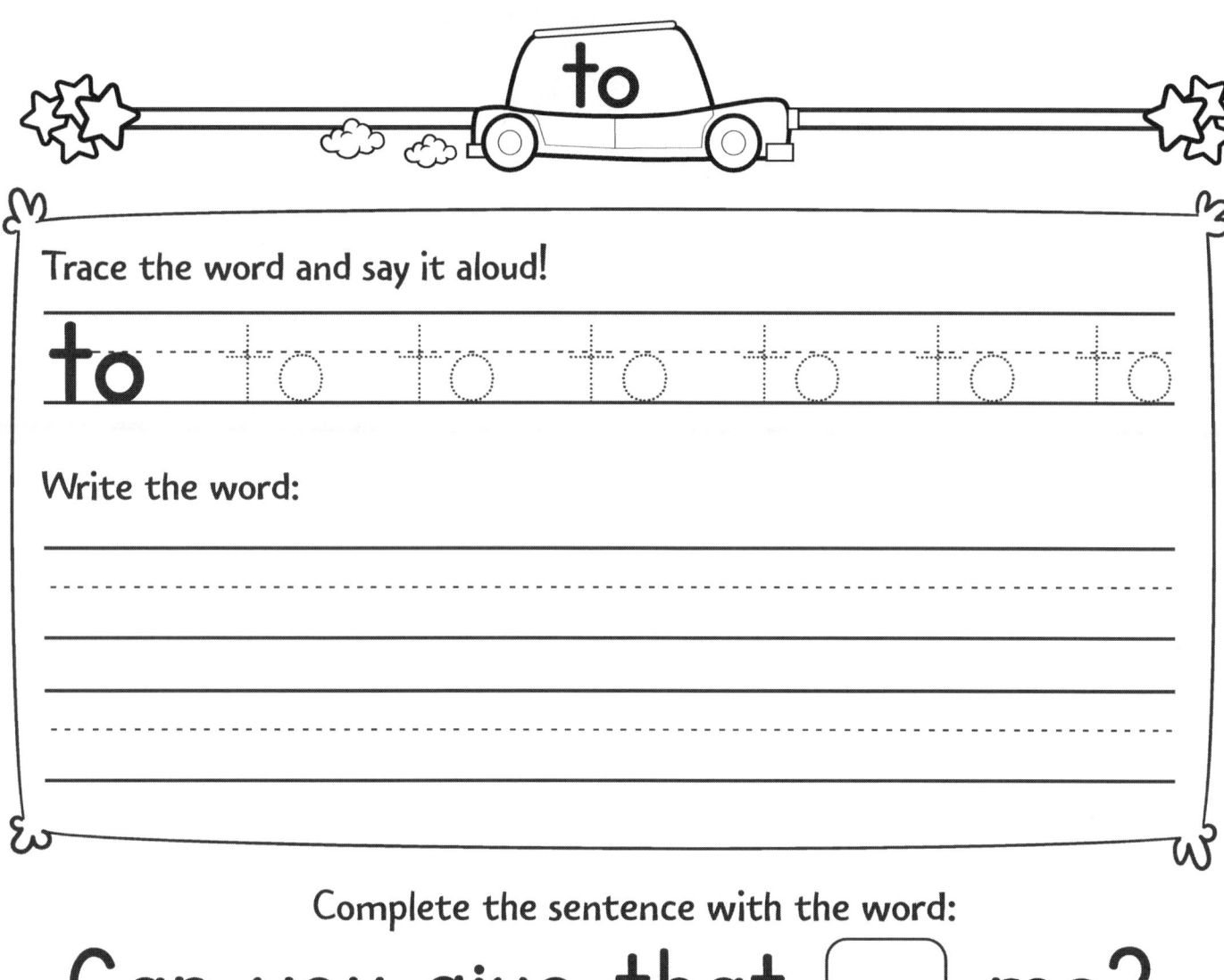

Trace the word and say it aloud!

to to to to to to to to to

Write the word:

Complete the sentence with the word:

Can you give that ☐ me?

Grab a crayon and color the shapes with the word!

to · this · to · to · the · they · to · that · to · there · try · to

under

Trace the word and say it aloud!

under under under

Write the word:

Complete the sentence with the word:

There are sharks _____ the water.

Grab a crayon and color the shapes with the word!

under · us · up · under · use · under · upon · unity · under · usual · under

up

Trace the word and say it aloud!

up　up　up　up　up　up　up

Write the word:

Complete the sentence with the word:

The airplane is ▢ __ __ .

Grab a crayon and color the shapes with the word!

want

Trace the word and say it aloud!

want want want want

Write the word:

Complete the sentence with the word:

Do you [___] to come?

Grab a crayon and color the shapes with the word!

want who want was went want we want want what well want

was

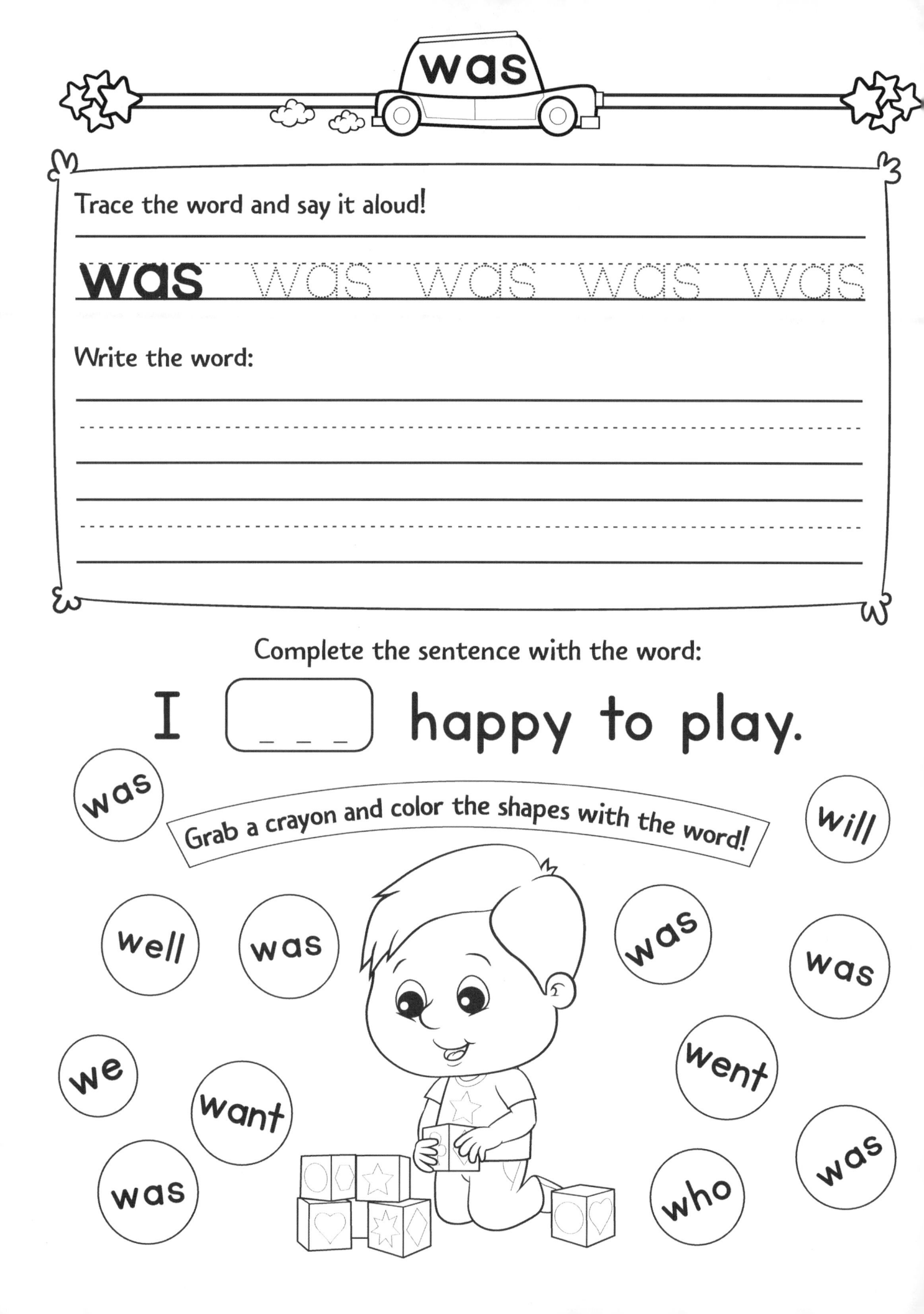

Trace the word and say it aloud!

was was was was was

Write the word:

Complete the sentence with the word:

I [___] happy to play.

Grab a crayon and color the shapes with the word!

was · will · well · was · was · was · we · went · want · was · who · was

we

Trace the word and say it aloud!

we we we we we

Write the word:

Complete the sentence with the word:

☐ are pirates!

Grab a crayon and color the shapes with the word!

we • went • we • well • was • we • who • we • we • will • what • we

well

Trace the word and say it aloud!

well well well well well

Write the word:

_____

Complete the sentence with the word:

I did [___] on my work.

Grab a crayon and color the shapes with the word!

we, well, was, well, well, who, what, will, well, well, well, with

went

Trace the word and say it aloud!

went went went went

Write the word:

Complete the sentence with the word:

I ⬚ swimming.

Grab a crayon and color the shapes with the word!

what

Trace the word and say it aloud!

what what what what

Write the word:

Complete the sentence with the word:

_ _ _ _ are you doing?

Grab a crayon and color the shapes with the word!

we · what · what · well · what · what · who · what · will · went · what · with

where

Trace the word and say it aloud!

where   where   where

Write the word:

Complete the sentence with the word:

[_ _ _ _ _] are you going?

Grab a crayon and color the shapes with the word!

we · will · well · who · where · where · where · what · where · went · where · where

who

Trace the word and say it aloud!

who   who   who   who

Write the word:

Complete the sentence with the word:

____ wants to play outside?

Grab a crayon and color the shapes with the word!

we   who   who   what   with   who   went   will   who   well   who

will

Trace the word and say it aloud!

will will will will will will

Write the word:

Complete the sentence with the word:

_____ you be my friend?

Grab a crayon and color the shapes with the word!

we · will · will · will · well · will · with · who · will · went · will · what

with

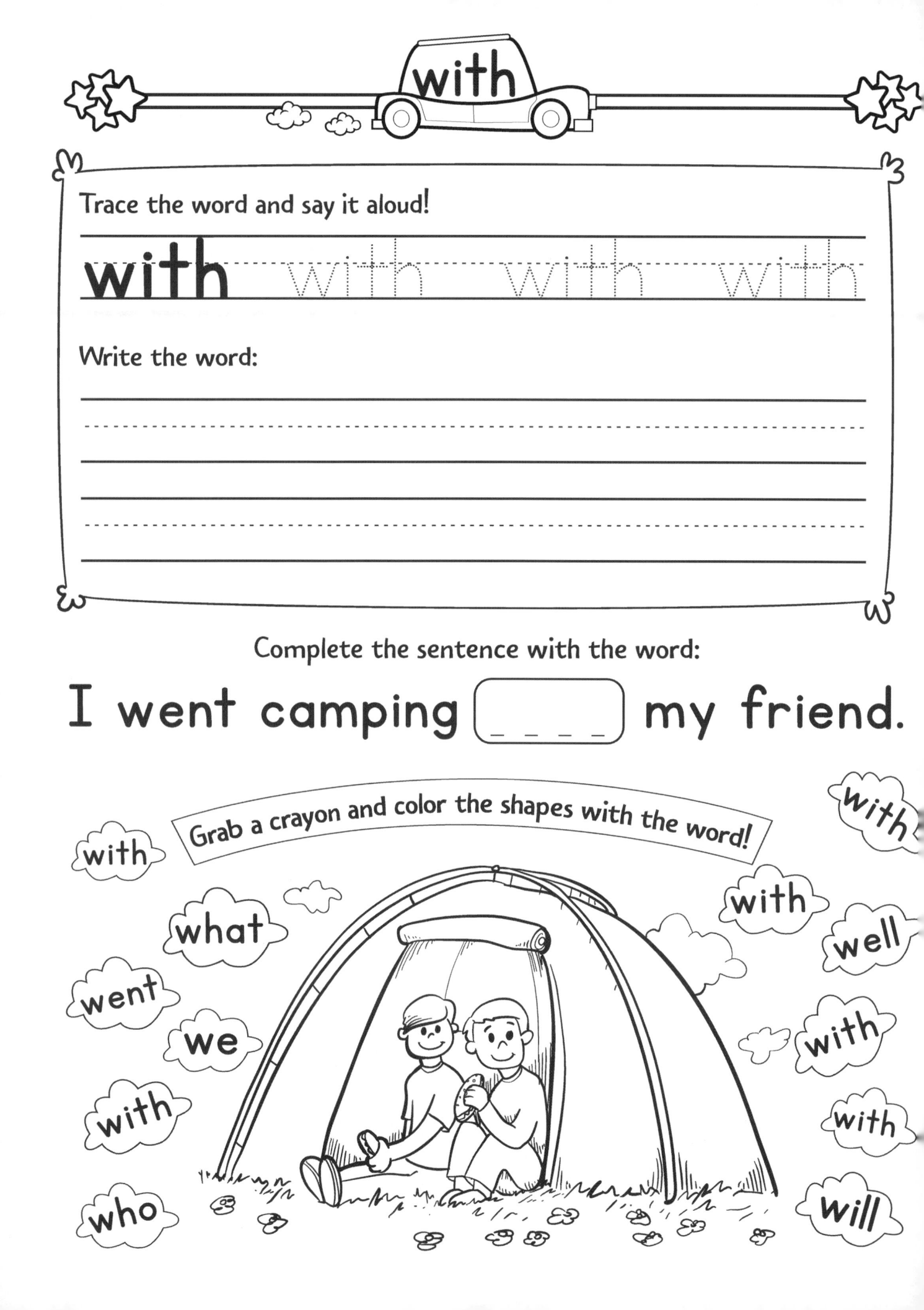

Trace the word and say it aloud!

with   with   with   with

Write the word:

Complete the sentence with the word:

I went camping ____ my friend.

Grab a crayon and color the shapes with the word!

with, what, went, we, with, who, with, well, with, with, will

yes

Trace the word and say it aloud!

yes   yes   yes   yes   yes

Write the word:

Complete the sentence with the word:

[_ _ _], I did it!

Grab a crayon and color the shapes with the word!

you   yes   yay   yard   year   yes   yes   yam   yes   yes   yeah   yes

you

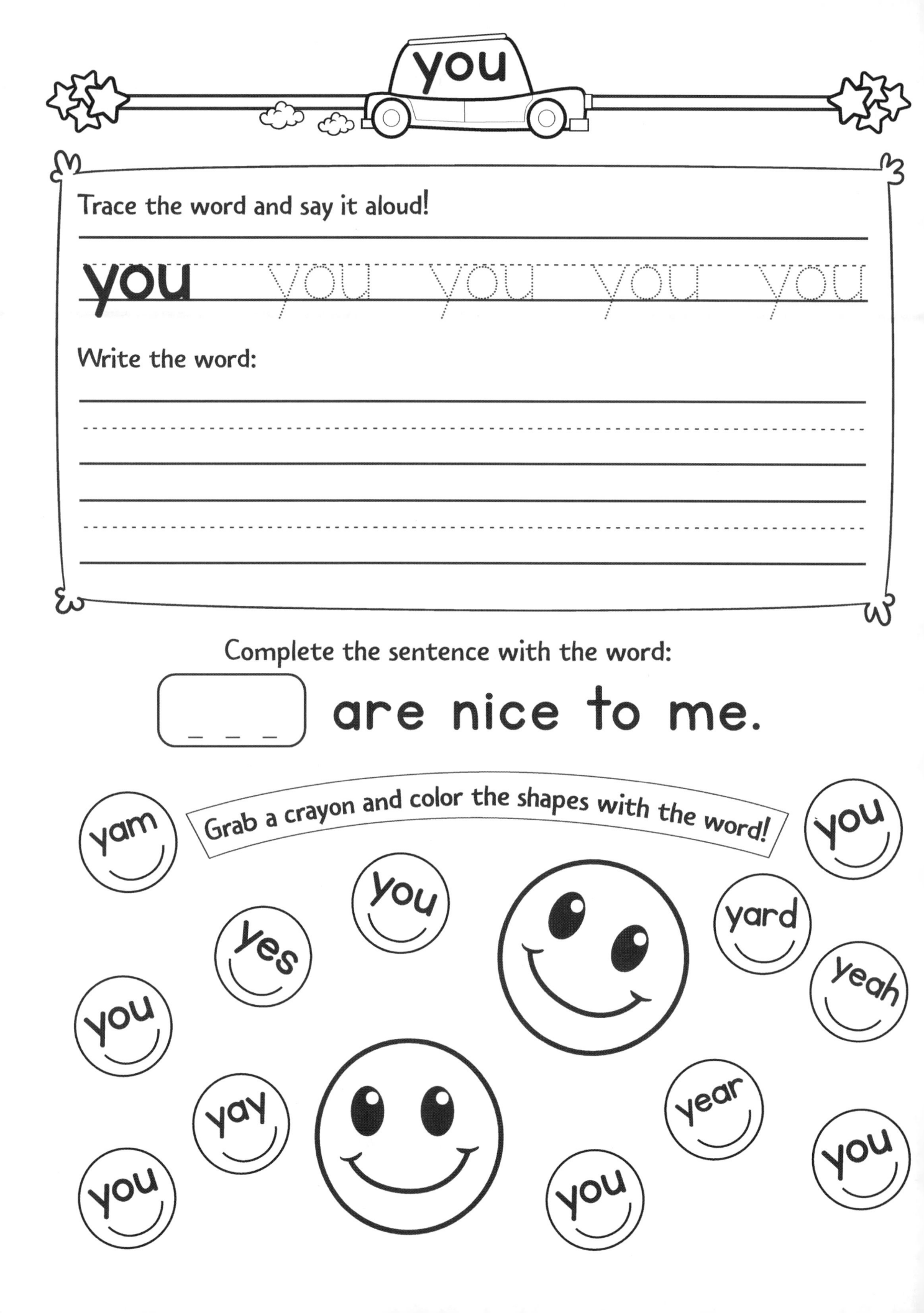

Trace the word and say it aloud!

you   you   you   you   you

Write the word:

Complete the sentence with the word:

_____ are nice to me.

Grab a crayon and color the shapes with the word!

yam · you · you · yard · yeah · yes · you · yay · year · you · you · you

Cut Out These Flash Cards for More Practice Fun!

one	two
three	four
five	red
blue	yellow
green	black

six	seven
eight	nine
ten	white
brown	purple
pink	orange

a	all
am	an
and	are
at	ate
away	be

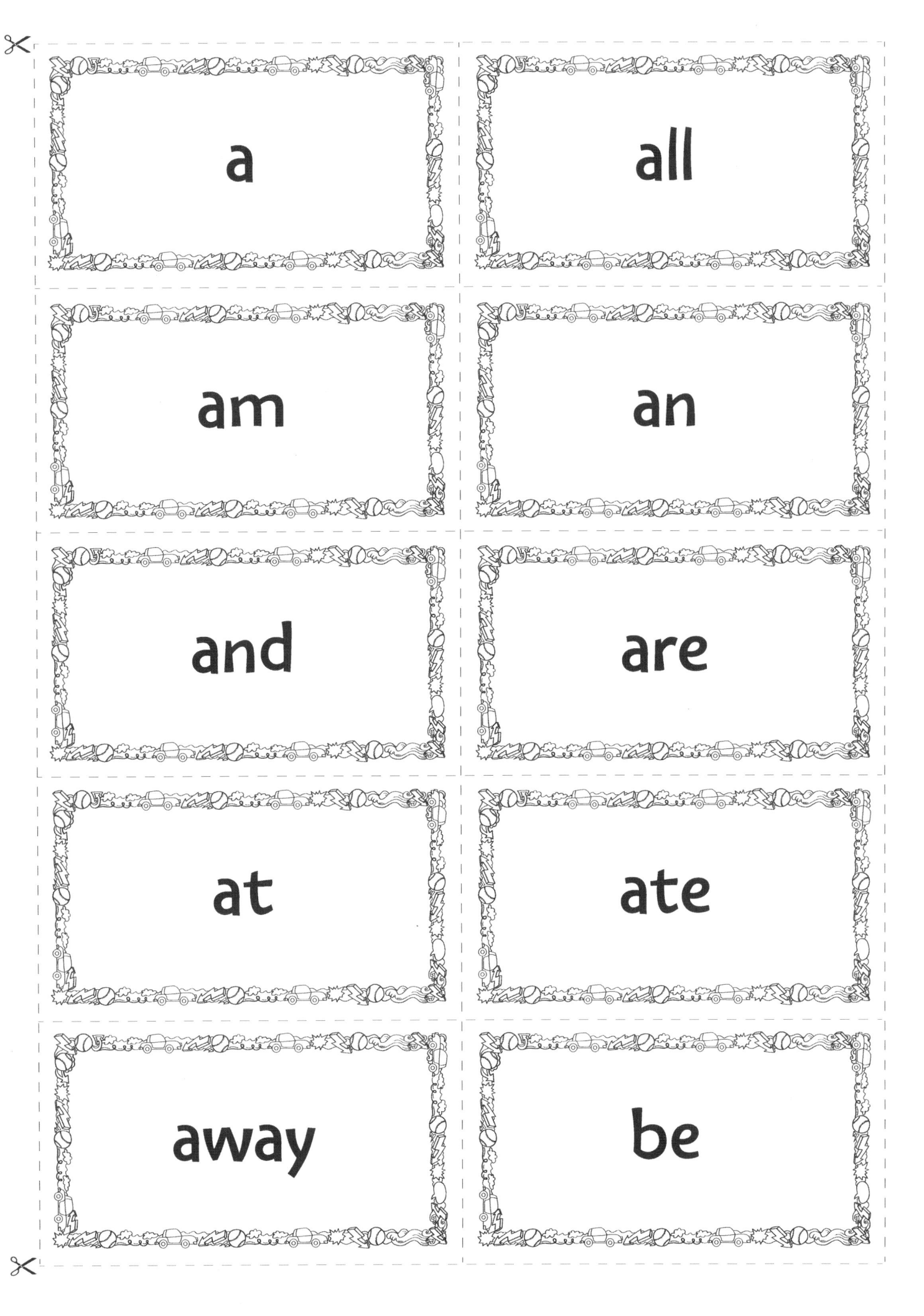

big	but
came	can
come	did
do	down
eat	find

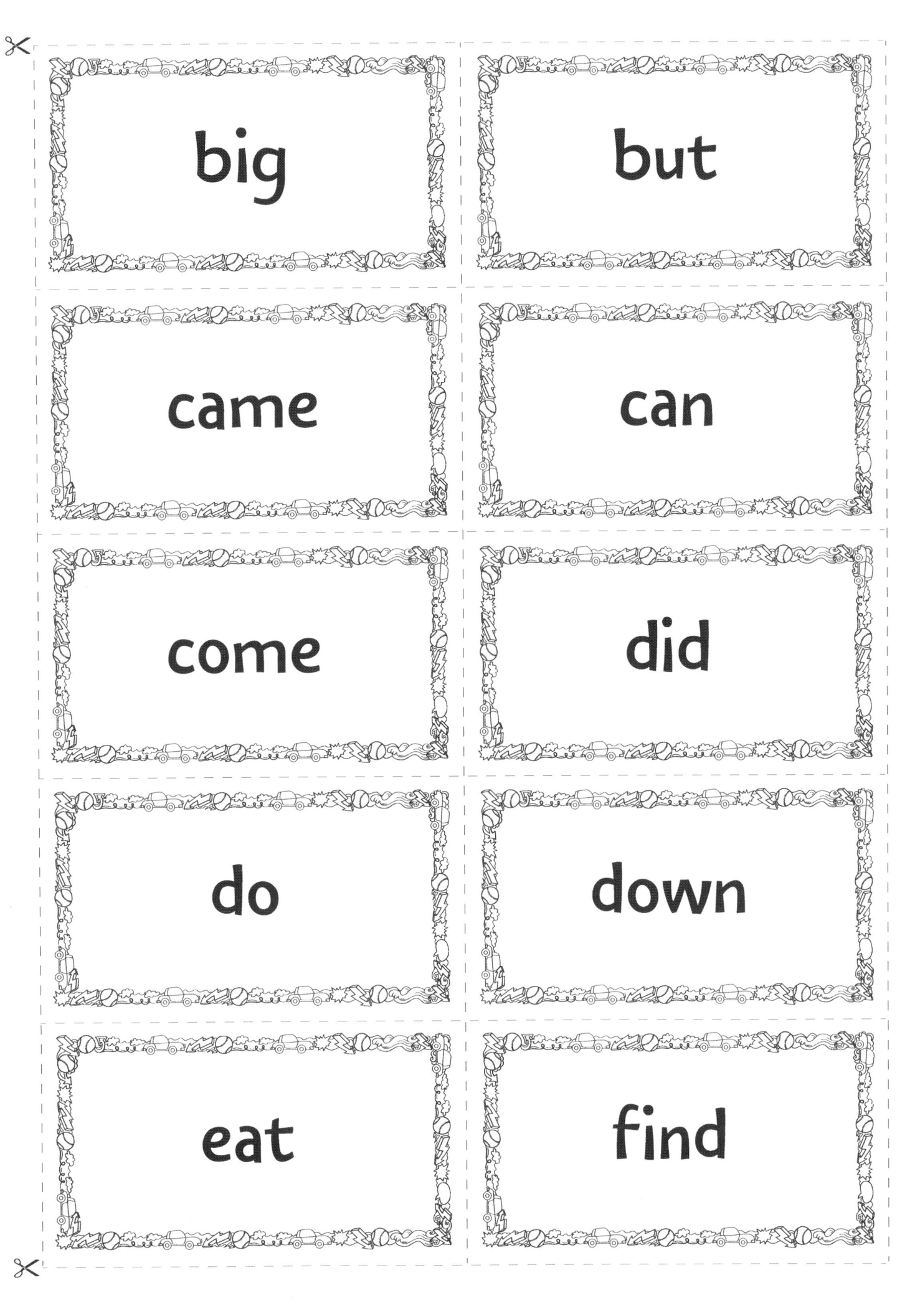

for	get
go	good
have	he
help	here
I	in

into	is
it	jump
like	little
look	make
me	my

new	no
not	now
on	our
out	play
please	pretty

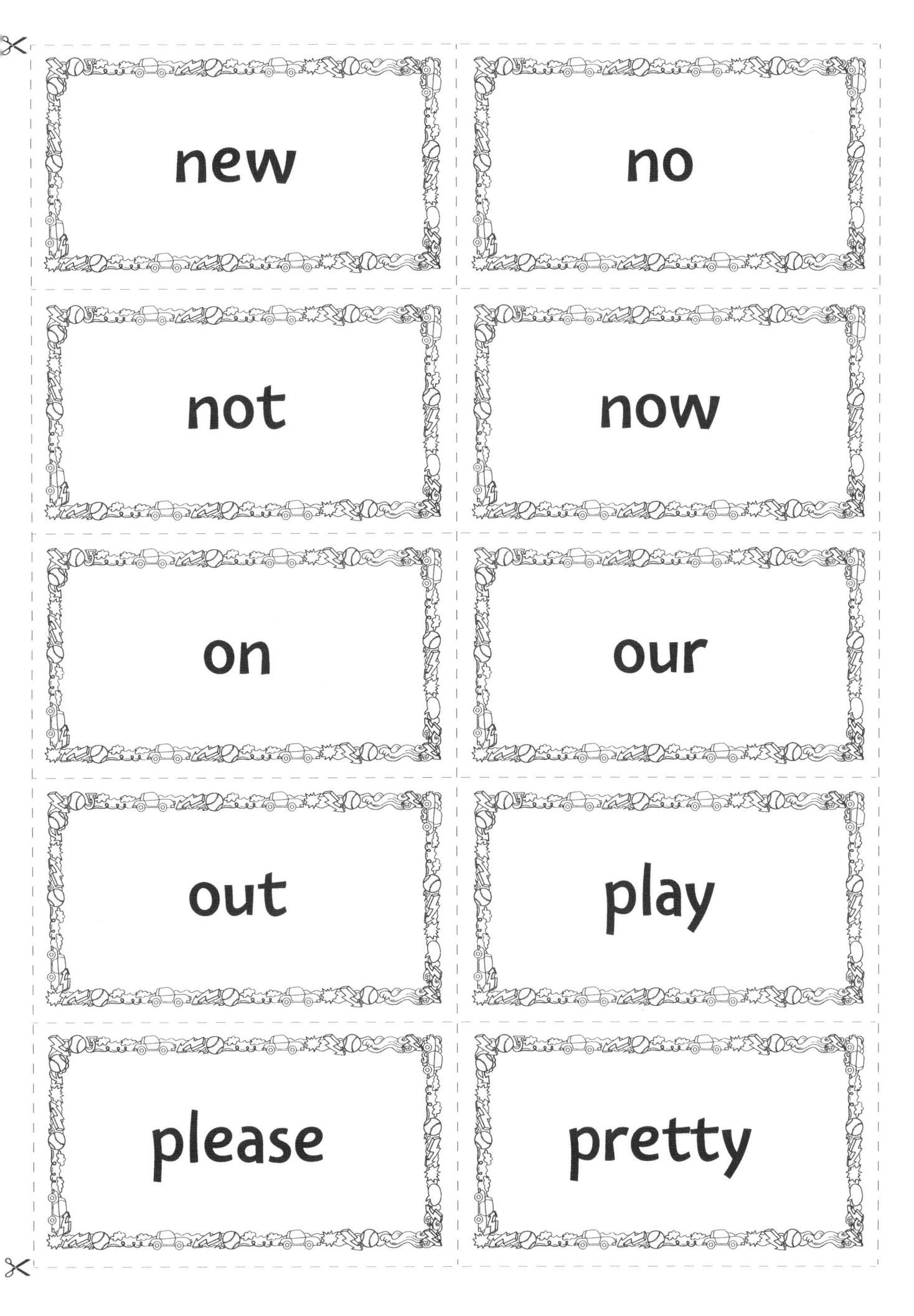

ran	ride
run	said
saw	say
see	she
so	soon

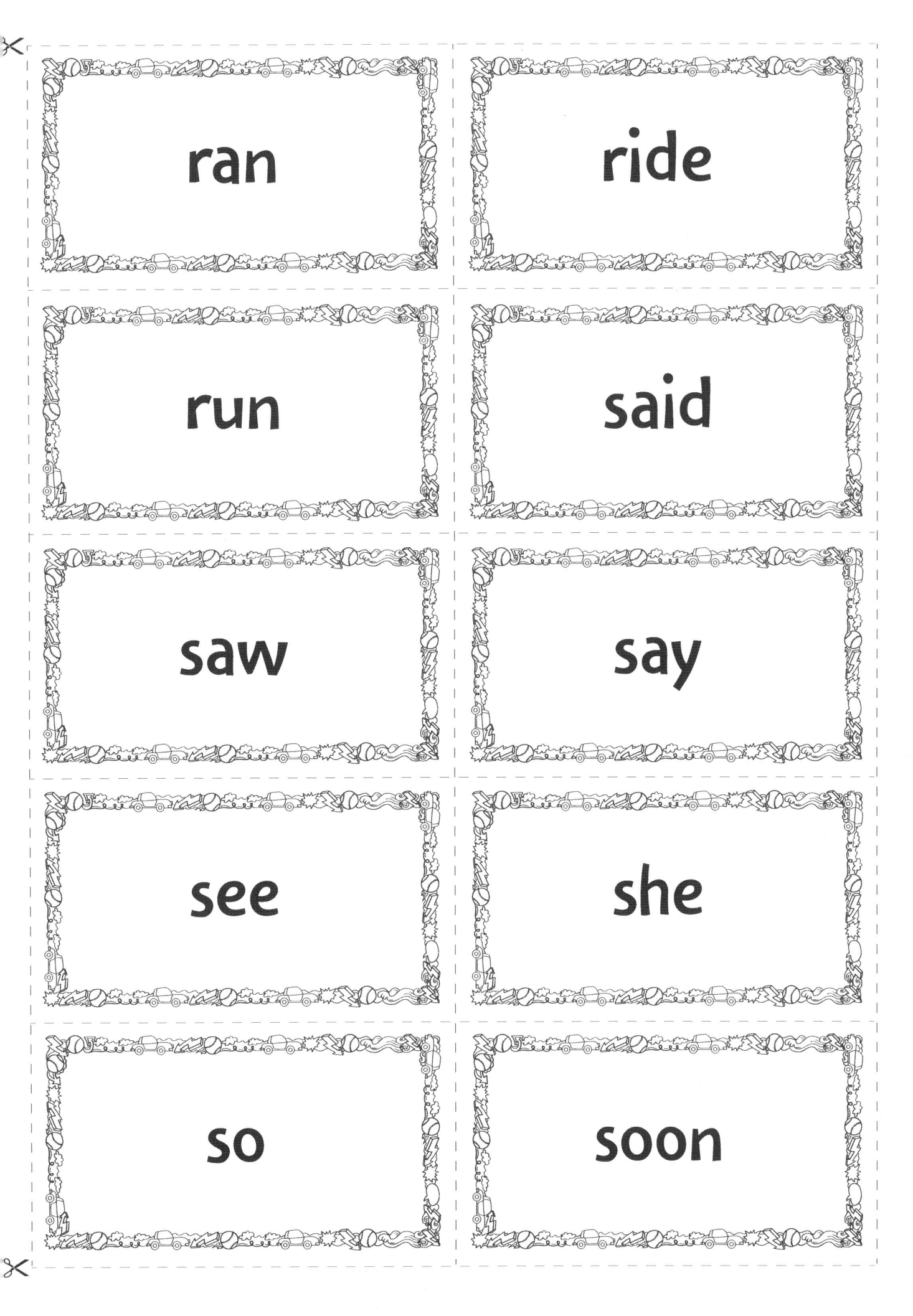

that	the
there	they
this	to
under	up
want	was

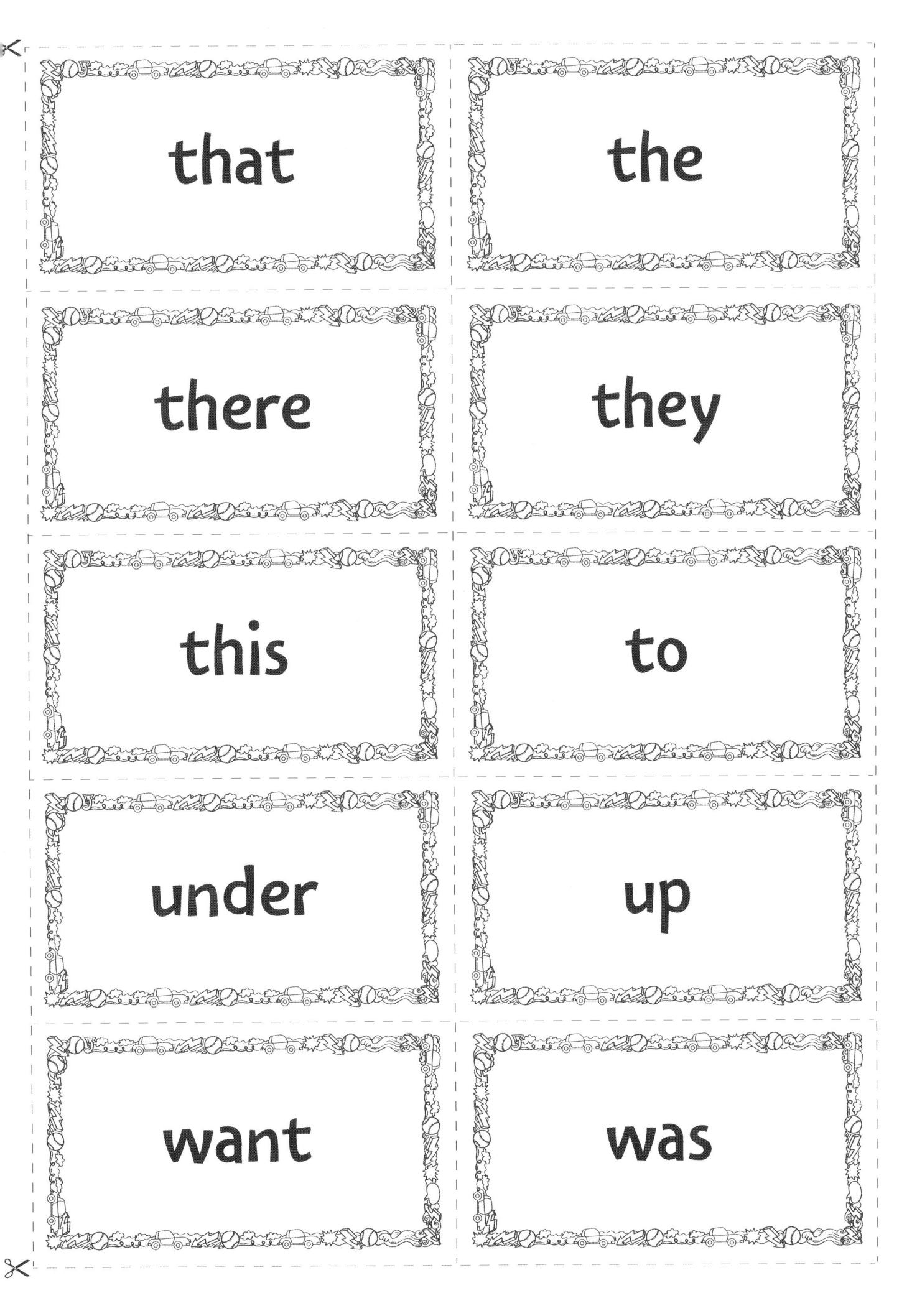

we	well
went	what
where	who
will	with
you	yes

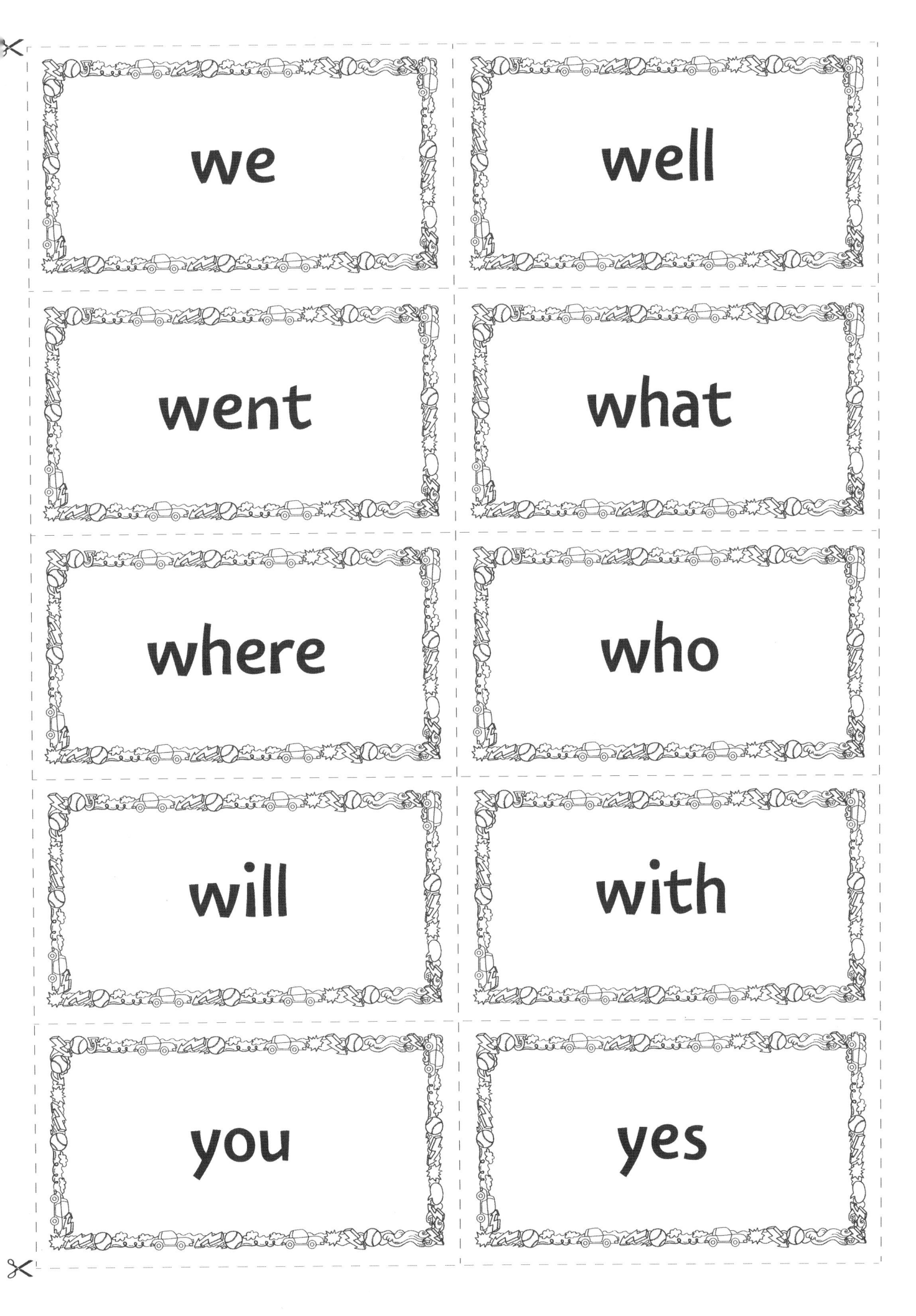

Congratulations!

You are a
Sight Word Superstar!
You can read 100 sight words!

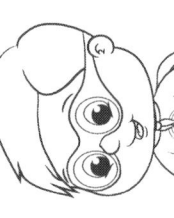

_____ _____
Date   Signature